ORDEAL BY
FIRE

a memoir

Rita Nayar

We acknowledge the support of the Canada Council for the Arts for our publishing program. We also acknowledge support from the Government of Ontario through the Ontario Arts Council and the Ontario Media Development Corporation Book Initiative.

The Canada Council | Le Conseil des Arts
for the Arts | du Canada

ONTARIO ARTS COUNCIL
CONSEIL DES ARTS DE L'ONTARIO

Cover designed by David Drummond

Edited by M G Vassanji

National Library of Canada Cataloguing in Publication

Nayar, Rita, 1952-
        Ordeal by fire / by Rita Nayar.

ISBN 1-894770-10-2

1. Nayar, Rita, 1952- 2. East Indian women--Canada--Biography.
3. Wives--India--Biography. I. Title.

FC106.S66Z7 2003   305.48'891411071'092   C2003-905786-0

Printed in Canada by Coach House Printing

TSAR Publications
P. O. Box 6996, Station A
Toronto, Ontario M5W 1X7
Canada

www.tsarbooks.com

For Nina and Vijay
Companions of my life and the darlings of my heart
You were there for me though you did not know it then

Contents

One

Early Years

ORDEAL BY FIRE

A Rajasthani Heritage

Udaipur, my birthplace in the southwest corner of
Rajasthan, is a beautiful lake town in northwestern India,
with a Maharaja's palace prominent on the lake's still
waters. Many kingdoms have existed in this large, desert state, and
there are a multitude of stories told in song about its kings and
queens, that captured my heart as a child. In these songs, the spoken language was accorded the utmost respect and upheld an
implicit code of the highest ethics, especially in regards to the relationships between men and women. The women were brave and
loyal, with poise and elegance that complemented perfectly their
courage and their devotion to the men they loved. These lyrical
landscapes of the sagas were drenched in color: women in
turquoise blues, bright fuchsias, and fiery oranges; men riding tall
camels wearing red *bandhani safas* on their heads.

There was one particular song, based on a true story, that cap-
tivated me and in later years became the cornerstone for my inspiration in difficult times. It dates from the days when wives would
throw themselves on their husbands' funeral pyres to save themselves from the dishonor of being captured and made concubines;
even captured women in most cases would rather take their own
lives by other means. The ballad is sung somewhat like prose, by
a single high male voice, with force and conviction. A young
woman has just married a prince. They have just gone to the bed-
chamber on their wedding night when the bugle blows, calling
him to war. He does not want to go; confused about what he
should do, he sits awhile on the side of the bed, his head in his
hands. His new bride cannot contain her outrage at this indecision. "Give me your sword," she taunts him, "and I will go to war.
You sit at home and wear my bangles" (an idiom for calling someone a coward). Upon hearing this, the prince jumps up, saddles his
horse and rides off. The music reaches a crescendo—and the

3

receding sound of the bugle mingles with the clatter of the horse's hooves. On the battlefield, he is plagued by thoughts of his young bride and sends a messenger to bring back a token of her affection. When the messenger reaches the young bride and conveys her husband's request, she replies, "Here, take this!"

The messenger runs to his master with a platter in both hands. On the platter is the bride's head—a token meant to remind her husband to perform his duty without the distracting thoughts of her that can only cause his death. Of course, in the end the prince does win the war and his resolute bride becomes his *devi* (goddess).

This song would make me cry. The young bride's selflessness had protected both her new husband and herself, for his death was certain, given that he could think of nothing else but her. There was a fearlessness in her that few could claim today and that I deeply admired as a girl. Even though I could never understand the words thoroughly, for it was sung in a local dialect, the sound and feel of the narrative were laden with passionate moments that spoke to my heart.

Also in Rajasthan, about fifty miles outside of Jodhpur, in the town of Merta, is the temple of Meera. She was a great saint and poet who struggled against all obstacles to devote her entire life to her beloved, Lord Krishna. Her poetry tells the story of the mystical love between her and her Lord. What poetry it was, Meera dancing rapturously with anklets on her feet, or waiting by the banks of the river to meet her beloved, her heart aching with love! Meera was another legendary figure who inspired me.

My father was born in a room adjacent to Meera's temple in the town where my grandfather lived as the city magistrate. His gift of a clock still hangs on one of the temple walls. It is a small temple in the heart of the city and the road to the temple is about the width of a modern car. Inside the temple is the statue of Krishna in his Charbhuja (four-handed) form, while Meerabai stands near the inside entrance with her stringed instrument. When I was a young teen we would visit Jodhpur, and I waited eagerly to visit the temple, to walk barefoot on the cool, black and white checkered marble floor.

I feel lucky to have been born into this lovely land, famous throughout India for its tales of royal splendor, courage and honor. Even though we left India when I was eight, my early exposure to the traditions and folklore of my homeland meant that they would remain in me always, and I cherish my pride in Rajasthan. The images and stories I absorbed as a child would stay deep within my consciousness, and I would embrace the noble ideals of my lineage by trying to live up to their lofty standards. They have instilled in me the gift of a deep-rooted instinct of courage and spirituality.

My Family

I remember standing in the doorway of the train, dwarfed by my father, as we began our journey to go abroad and spend our life outside India. He had what seemed like hundreds of garlands around his neck. The yellow, strong-petalled marigolds seemed quietly to reflect the strength that I saw in my father; and the delicate fragrance of the flowers, his inner strength. Known to the world as Dr Madhav Mal Mehta, having completed his DLit after his PhD, he was leaving behind all his beloved friends, employees, and coworkers at the Ministry of Economics of the state of Madhya Pradesh to take up a prestigious and greatly sought-after job with the United Nations. Unaware that I should be immensely proud of him, I was happy just to stand beside him and bask in the glory that was being showered upon him. We were going to live abroad, in Burma, and my spirit was already attuned to the excitement of the future.

Baba, as I called him, was a thoughtful man, and I always think of him in his usual pose, sitting on a chair somewhere, resting his face on his index finger and thumb. People always said that we had the same oval cut of the face, the same quiet demeanor and mannerisms, the same philosophic absentmindedness; and yet, Baba and I hardly talked. In fact, Baba hardly spoke to anyone. He lived in his own thoughts, far away from the crowded push and pull of everyday life. Possessions did not possess him, and wealth did not make him wealthy.

As a teenager, I would sneak into his study to peek through the few books he had. One of these was Tagore's *Gitanjali*, in which he had underlined some of the passages in red. Tagore, the poet-philosopher who won the Nobel Prize for literature for his famous composition *Gitanjali*, evoked in me the most sentimental feelings of beauty and mysticism and left me with an appreciation for the deeply philosophical nature of life. I was particularly fond of the thirteenth verse:

The song that I came to sing remains unsung to this day.
I have spent my days in stringing and in unstringing my instrument.

I remember vividly a day in Kashmir, where we had gone for holidays when I was sixteen. I was lying on the floor near Baba's feet in our houseboat, which did not have sufficient room to stretch out, when he began to softly stroke my hair. It was the height of demonstrative love from him and somehow I understood this perfectly and felt the quiet harmony that existed between us. Without word or gesture, we had shared a special moment.

My mother (given the masculine name Ajeet, because her father had wanted a boy) was a gorgeous woman with a heart-shaped face. She married Baba when she was thirteen and he was twenty. It was an arranged marriage, according to the custom of those days. They had been engaged when they were only five and twelve.

Ma would sometimes fondly recall stories about her childhood. Her mother, whom she described as the most beautiful woman in

Jodhpur, died of TB when Ma was only seven and her younger siblings were five, three, and one. Her father never remarried and left the task of nurturing the young ones to the women of the household—mainly Ma. As a child, Ma was not allowed to learn to read or write, so she would sneak books into the kitchen, hiding them under her clothes, and try to learn there all by herself. Baba used to visit her father's shop once in a while, and she had been chosen as his bride even though she was from a different community. She was a Jain, and he a Marwari from the service class. She had felt very fortunate to have married an educated man.

Of course, when Baba married her, he encouraged her to learn, which she did, and she went on to become an educated, sophisticated woman. She was neat, organized, and precise and never gave in to rumor or gossip. Nor did I ever hear her complain about her circumstances or her fate. I always believed, though, that Ma's tough childhood had drained her of emotion and the ability to find happiness. Perhaps because she seemed so aloof, so content within herself, I felt that she needed nothing. I don't know why this made me feel sorry for her, but often as a teenager I agonized over what I sensed was her deep-rooted loneliness. Although Baba was my idol, I could hardly picture him being romantic and demonstrative, and I felt that she, like many women, needed so much more than her husband could give. It was an aspect of their private life I could never reconcile.

Ma would sometimes talk about how she never believed in God as such, even though she would occasionally indulge in telling us a few anecdotes from the epic *Ramayana*. As a Jain, she did not worship idols, and so we did not have an elaborate altar at home as normal Hindu families did.

I have a sister, Ranjana Didi, who is four years older than I. She went away to boarding school in Gwalior, a city in central India, when I was about four or five. Baba would be transferred from city to city and it was common to send children to reputable boarding schools for a stable education. It was never easy for me to understand Didi, who was segregated from the family so early in life. Her prolonged stays at school hindered our ability to share and relate to each other. I saw her for only a few months every year, when she would visit us for her summer holidays. I am sure that the repercussions of her living away from home did not occur to either of my parents, but for the two of us it took time and effort to establish a sisterly bond.

We had a servant, Ramu, for whom I had great affection. He had been with us long before I was born. Baba had hired a fourteen-year-old lad called Ramu from a neighboring village to help around the house while he was teaching at Allahabad University. Later, we took Ramu abroad with us, where he found his life partner. He was short, but not plump, with a happy round face and chubby cheeks, and his shyness made it difficult for him to look anyone in the eye. Perhaps he was kindest to me because it was I who liked him the most and often talked to him. He enthusiastically told me stories about ghosts who had their feet turned inwards and who troubled people on the farms at night. His slight stutter seemed to enhance his sincerity, and I listened to him with great absorption.

With utmost respect, Ramu would keep a distance of several feet from all of us, and he performed his duties faithfully through all my years into adulthood, and I never felt anything but true devotion from him. In later years I lost track of him and tried to find him. When I came to know where he was, he had recently passed away in Allahabad. Although I rarely cry, his death brought tears to my eyes. His worth was far above his station in life.

My brother, Rajiv, is four years younger than me. He was a lanky kid with a sensitive smile and gentle mannerisms. I was very close to him; with Didi away most of the time, there were only the two of us with our parents. Raj was always a quiet soul, and we could spend time together in total ease, without chatting, content in our common surroundings and busy with our own activities.

The First Years Abroad: Burma

Memories of Burma, now known as Myanmar, come back in bits and pieces, threads that weave into the patterns of my life. I was nine when we came to Burma and I recall it first as a fine landscape of tall, yellow laburnum trees hanging low, reaching for the ground. We lived in an apartment in the capital city of Rangoon. It did not take long before I had a few friends in our small, enclosed compound that housed four or five low buildings. Hazel, my Anglo-Burmese best friend next door, taught me how to ride a bike on the uneven grounds, which were covered with heavy roots and fresh yellow petals. Hazel's father, an engineer, was British and her mother, Burmese. Her older sister, Marilyn, who was seeing Pierre, the son of the French ambassador, first made me conscious of differences in cultures. I remember how Marilyn treated us "little ones" to a tour of the grand house of the French Embassy, where she had gone to meet Pierre. Hazel and I softly tiptoed into what seemed like a gigantic mansion, awed by pretty, delicate things the likes of which we had never seen before. I dared not disturb their settings in the slightest. Marilyn looked gorgeous in her sarong and angi, and I marveled at the charm and beauty of her perfectly chiseled face. What, I wondered, did she see in the ambassador's son? I had seen him a couple of times in his leather jacket, sitting astride his motorbike. She seemed worthy of a king!

Like other children in the compound, many from Israel, and others from different parts of the world, I attended the International School of Rangoon. It was torture for me. The principal had skipped me two grades, but my knowledge of English was far too limited, and I was not sufficiently adept at American history or the new math. Coming from Indian convent schools, I found the culture shock from this new school environment too great, and I struggled to keep up. I can still hear my math teacher telling me, "Think twice before you speak!", making me feel like the dumbest child in school. To this day I remember her words, and even though I occasionally take her wise advice, back then I blamed only myself for my inabilities. It never occurred to me that shortsightedness on the part of the school, or the insensitivity of some of the teachers, contributed to my feelings of worthlessness. Instead, I came to detest myself for my ineptitude. Worse still, I was sure that Ma thought I was stupid.

Several times our family went to visit Buddhist temples, the well-known pagodas of Burma. I was truly moved by the statues of Buddha, who looked so peaceful with his gentle smile. I loved his face and his body, which was beautiful and golden. His eyes could see, but they saw nothing. His heart could hear, and all it heard was an enchanted silence. He had long earlobes, just like Baba, and I loved him and Baba with the same unquestioning love. I was sure that what Buddha said was true: "There is nothing in this world that is not worth giving up for peace." And hadn't he given up everything—his whole kingdom, his wealth, his palace, his wife, and his child—all to attain harmony with the universe? How inspired he had been to search for the Truth, and he had not given up until he found it.

Being introverted and shy, I struggled to keep that spiritual peace and innocence in my being, but the real world had a way of creeping in and disturbing the serenity. I dreamt one night that a couple of soldiers had shot both my parents in front of our apartment. It was a dream so shocking that I have never forgotten how vivid and real it seemed. Shortly afterwards, our driver threw up blood, went to hospital, and died of tuberculosis. One morning, a few months after my tenth birthday, I woke up to find my sheets full of blood. I ran to Ma in a panic and told her that I, too, needed to go to the hospital. I was sure I was dying. "No," she told me, "you're fine." I had just become a woman.

Our *aayah* (nanny), Ratna, unwittingly revealed to me another aspect of life's brutality. From time to time, she would take Raj and me for a walk around the block and buy us small salted lemon cubes from a corner stand, which we would suck as we walked past the French Embassy. One day, she took us to her home, a small dingy room in a crowded alley in Rangoon, and there I caught a glimpse of her husband, a man who looked far too old for her. He was squatting on the floor and chewing on a stick, his teeth grinding inside as his stubble of a white beard moved in circles. I discovered later that he would abuse her when he drank. She somehow extricated herself from that marriage during the summer months before we left Rangoon. Discreetly, she and Ramu joined together as a couple. It made me happy to think of their courage. Did a bad marriage prevent you from searching for happiness? Ramu was so shy I could never have imagined him with a woman, but there they both were, beaming with embarrassment at the revelation of their union. They were going to come with us on our newly announced move to Thailand.

After two years in Burma, Baba had taken a long-term posting as Regional Director of ECAFE (Economic Commission for Asia and the Far East) in Bangkok. It was a good time to leave Burma, given that military government was turning the local population against Burmese Indians and expelling them. The Indians in Burma were mostly traders, having lived there for generations, and we had come to know them well. Now many had to leave the country empty handed.

In the Bustle of Bangkok

The bustle of life in the streets of Bangkok was a sharp contrast to the slow pace of Rangoon. The city was humid, and when the monsoons hit, the tall trees would sway wildly and throw sudden torrents of water on passersby. I loved the rains and the sweet smell of the earth, the heat rising from its parched surface as the first drops fell. Then the downpour came, and it felt as if the heavens were emptying out their anguish—as if in cleaning the world, they also cleansed themselves. Pour, pour, pour down on me. Drench my hair so that the drops fall off the ends, fall onto my eyelashes, into my mouth. Every drop just the right warmth. And then, the clearing of the skies came like a sigh of relief from the heavy heart of the heavens.

We lived at Soi Twelve, on Sukhumvit Road, at the end of a residential avenue. Ours was the sixth house, and it had two living rooms and the usual dining and kitchen area downstairs. Upstairs were three large bedrooms with many netted windows, and a huge round balcony the size of the three bedrooms put together. Like most houses this one was made completely of wood. Behind it was a three-roomed servant quarter. It was a gorgeous home. Sunlight streamed through the west-facing windows of the living room and my bedroom upstairs, and warmed the floors. My favorite parts of the house were the round balcony outside our bedrooms and the gray mosaic veranda outside our living room, where Raj and I hung around in the evenings. From there, I could see all the tropical flowers of our garden: the fragrant white frangipanis that I adored; the red bottlebrush; the jasmine; and the roses Ma had instructed the Thai gardener to plant along the winding driveway. Even though the garden was lovely, I still felt it needed something else to highlight its beauty; so I asked Ramu if he could make me a little pond with umbrella palms and white lilies around it. With great enthusiasm he built the pond right outside the front entrance of our house. And it was lovely.

Our street had trees on one side and houses on the other. Most of the girls in the neighborhood had parents in the diplomatic service who stayed a few years and moved on. Perhaps they also felt like me—a gust of wind that hesitates at every destination and finally dissolves without settling anywhere. My friend Alka, whose Dad was also with the UN, and I would explore construction sites—I once fell through a plumbing hole on the fifth floor and got stuck! Sometimes her father took us swimming at the Dusit Thani Hotel, and when we came home we would cook spaghetti together. There was the daughter of the First Secretary at the

Indian Embassy, Poonam, to whom I ultimately presented my collection of articles on astronomy and space travel that I had painstakingly assembled in the days when I wanted to be an astronaut; Ilze, from New Zealand, who promised to keep in touch, but didn't; little Angie, whose father was fighting in Vietnam and who would offer licks of her ice cream to Latka, Ramu's dog. There was a sweet young woman from Malaysia named Usha, who had three little children and a mole on her chin. The subdued smile on her face could not hide the great sadness I sensed in her wide eyes.

One of my closest relationships was with my next-door neighbor, whom I called Aunty Khan. She was the same age as Ma and very artistically talented. I was fascinated by her creations of papier mâché, her dolls clothes, and her flower arrangements. Her sitar was my first introduction to Indian classical music. Though in our home we spoke a comfortable mix of Hindi and English, in time, I came to understand from Aunty Khan the nuances, in speech and music, of Urdu—a charmingly poetic language which she spoke impeccably.

My memories of that time in Bangkok, though, are linked most vividly with my discovery of my mother's personality. Ma usually lay in bed, reading, except when she was bustling around trying to supervise the household. She had an insatiable thirst for information about the world and would go through journals and magazines from cover to cover, initializing them at the back with the symbol @, which stood for her name. Ma seemed quite content to be on her own. She did not have close friends, and I can't remember her ever talking on the phone. In fact, our telephone was kept in the upstairs hallway where there was no chair to sit on, discouraging long conversations. Very rarely did our family have visitors, and we never visited friends—as a family or individually. This was very unusual by Indian standards. It is from Ma that I learned to be happy on my own, and this has become an invaluable and natural element of my adult life.

After school, my brother Raj and I would throw ourselves on to the master bed in her air-conditioned room, which was such a relief from the humidity and heat we had experienced on the way home. In the very hot summer afternoons we would play chess there, while Ma took her nap on the other side of the huge bed. Raj and I shared a room, and peace engulfed our little world when we spent time together. I would lie on my bed reading or listening to the radio while Raj would be totally engrossed with Lego, making all kinds of four-wheeled inventions. There was a game we used to play before going to bed: I would ask Raj to tell me the percentage of his sleepiness, and I would tell him mine. The higher number would be the lucky one. I can never remember fighting with him. He listened to me, and I never took advantage of him. I was taught that one should listen to an elder, but the elder should never take advantage. I made no demands on him and felt guilty even asking him to fetch me a drink of water.

Without being aware of it, Ma indulged Raj emotionally. Every night when she came to our room to say goodnight, she would lie down beside him. I can remember our white mosquito nets that waved about due to the fan whirring above us; the lingering smell of Flit, a chemical spray for mosquitoes; and I was aware of the extra attention my mother gave my brother. It did not really bother me. I must have rationalized that he was the youngest child and needed more care; besides, I loved my brother. He had a deep passion for music, and the lyrics that he invented to the popular tunes of the day made me roll with laughter. Pretending to be oblivious to my state, he would go on singing his silly songs with a serious face. We shared a love for all things silly, and our similar sense of humor was a mystery to others—except Ma. She and I could laugh until tears rolled down our cheeks and our stomachs hurt. It was wonderful to see Ma lighten up—a sight that we did not experience very often! Once, Raj and I were telling Ma that mothers couldn't summersault and have fun when, suddenly, she sat up erect on the bed and before we knew it turned summersaults—not once, but twice! She couldn't turn down a dare. She had a wild but innocent streak in her that I like to think I have managed to inherit.

I always felt that Ma harbored traces of unrequited love from her past. When I was eleven, we traveled by train from Calcutta to Benares to visit the holy sanctuaries during one of our summer holidays in India. Seated with us in our compartment, across from my berth, was a middle-aged woman traveling alone. At one of the stops, a tall, exceptionally fine-looking man entered our compartment. There was a chemistry and attraction between the man and the woman that I immediately noticed. It was obvious from their intense and silent gazes that he had turned up only to be with her. And then, as the train clipped steadily along accompanied by the occasional screeching of the wheels, she stretched out on the berth, and her head had lay on his lap for the duration of the time between two stations. It appeared to be a secret rendezvous and the way they met made me wonder what complications they were encountering or what they were trying to hide. At the time, I had simply watched them through sleepy, half-closed eyelids, but later I would often think about them. Occasionally they must have snatched an hour or two to find loving comfort in each other's arms. I was happy at the thought of their romantic rendezvous, even though its unfulfilled state must also have created profound agonies for them. I am grateful to have tolerance and understanding for the delicate and subtle intricacies of human existence that only such experiences can teach. I had wished at the time Ma, like the mysterious woman on the train, had somehow also experienced feelings of romantic love.

Our home life was quiet and peaceful. My parents did not fight—not even the remote semblance of an argument escaped from their lips, whether in dealing with us kids or with each other. "When you have children of your own," Ma advised me, "never fight in front of them." When she told me this I began to wonder whether Ma and Baba truly had a peaceful relationship, or whether they had made a deliberate decision to refrain from dramatics in front of the children. I never let those doubts get the better of me, though, and opted for the former possibility. We certainly grew up wearing rose-tinted glasses. The only time Raj and I prepared for discord was during the time leading up to Didi's summer homecoming from boarding school. "Now don't fight with her," my mother would warn us in Hindi as the summer approached. "She'll be home only two months, so let her have her way." We had no choice but to prepare ourselves for an altered lifestyle in the summer season. Boarding school had encouraged my sister to be assertive and independent, and my brother and I could see how differently my parents treated her, compared to the two of us. Didi certainly lay down the law for my brother and me. I, for one, didn't appreciate her intrusion, but I also knew that there was no doubt of her academic superiority and I needed her help with math and science; so I let her have her way.

When I was seven, I had been sent to the same boarding school as Didi, but she had complained about my being too much trouble for her to take care of, and I had been sent back home. She was eleven years old at the time, and I can understand her frustration at having to take responsibility for a younger sibling. But how fortunate for me; had I stayed in the sheltered and exclusive environment of the boarding school, I would not have experienced the varied world around me—experiences that have shaped me and are very dear to me now.

Even those experiences which unexpectedly altered my life forever.

The Diplomatic Life

Baba's job with the International Labor Organization involved him in the economic policies of the Asian and Far Eastern countries. He came from a working-class family, unlike either the *Marwaris*, the business class, or the *Rajputs*, the warriors, who are prevalent in Rajasthan. His father, Bahadur Mal Mehta, had been the district magistrate of Merta, and died when Baba was three. His mother had raised him and his five siblings on her own. Baba had worked his way up from being a university professor at Allahabad University. He received a fellowship to MIT (Massachusetts Institute of Technology), worked for the Indian government as the Director of Economics in the state of Madhya Pradesh, and then went on to a career with the United Nations. But he was humble in the extreme and devoid of worldly ambitions. He did, however, find enormous satisfaction in self-achievement. And there was no one, including the servants and the children, to whom he did not bow when he began a conversation. I cherish that image of him.

Because of Baba's position, he often received gifts—Japanese dolls in huge glass cases, Korean wall hangings, Chinese hand paintings and brocade figures, Russian music boxes, Egyptian vanity cases that looked like cigarette holders, Filipino napkins made of rice paper and matching seashell holders, gorgeous Indonesian batiks, Burmese lacquer work, and Thai silks. I loved the soft batiks and seashell work that mirrored the natural beauty inherent in the universe. But more enchanting for me was the respect that the bearers of these gifts had for Baba. Most of them were young recruits, and they displayed impeccable manners, humility, and grace.

From time to time, Baba would host office parties for his colleagues on our front lawn. I remember these cocktail parties since they were so different from the routine of our daily life. Our house would be transformed, with plenty of oysters and caviar, drinks, and multicolored cocktail cigarettes in the fancy black 555 tins. Plate after plate of Indian finger foods, savories with layers of pastries, and skewered meat were served by well-dressed attendants brought in for the occasion. Our lawn would be filled with the music of many lands and the accents of many languages. There would be the blurs and swathes of the colors and designs of dif-

17

ferent attires. I learnt how to say "how are you" and "thank you" in many languages. But particularly amusing to my teenage mind were the Russians, who would click their heels and kiss the back of my hand grandly as I smiled courteously, holding back my giggles but feeling grown-up all the same.

At those times, it did my heart good to know how different my mother was from the pretentious and heavily made-up other wives. Charming, refined, and elegant, Ma would make my father proud as he introduced her, calling her the feminine Anu, instead of Ajeet. He was grateful he never had to tell her to hurry up or worry about being late. Always very organized and in control, she was the perfect diplomat's wife.

Still, it was my father who held my imagination. In his study at home, wearing his white *banyan* (vest) and his khaki-colored pants, Baba would work continuously at his desk on weekends, getting up only when meals were ready. He was meticulous, and even his writing was tiny, exact, and detailed. I can still hear the clicking of his typewriter keys, the pauses while he thought, and the longer gaps accompanied by the whirring of the roller as he inserted new sheets of paper into place. I can still see the well-used sheets of carbon paper lying on his desk. Even the smell of Baba's cigarettes was pleasing to me, as he sat biting on the well-chewed holder. I do not know exactly what it was that fascinated me about him, but I do know that his quiet demeanor made me very peaceful and blended very well with my own pensive moods. I placed my own study table in Baba's study, close to the window that looked down on a jungle of overgrown plants and trees. Staring out the window, through the shrubbery, at the *klong* (canal) that lay beyond the walled boundaries of our house, I would gaze for hours at the murky green water. Wild, unkempt, and untouched, the view suited me just fine, this was my sanctuary where I could hope to feel some level of inspiration. Sometimes Baba would be in the study as I sat doing my school work, but most of the weekdays I would have the room to myself. I had been put back a grade in Bangkok, and school was no longer a problem for me. I was gaining confidence. My personality was taking root.

Summers in India: Beautiful Jodhpur and a Few Malevolent Encounters

The UN provided us with home leave, so we went to India every second summer and stayed in Jodhpur for several weeks. My uncles and aunts, with their numerous children, lived scattered across the city. Jodhpur is the second largest city in Rajasthan, and is famous for its magnificent forts and palaces—huge structures built mainly of pink stone, which now housed rare items like palanquins, pearl-embroidered maharajas' shoes, intricately carved swords' sheaths, and lavishly upholstered royal howdahs meant for elephant-travel. I loved going to Jodhpur. We would take the overnight train from Delhi. Our family of four always had our own compartment, and I would stare out its window, watching the landscape change to dry, pink desert. Its sparseness and unending vastness held a mysterious beauty for me, especially at dusk. The desert was an ocean of sand, quiet and haunting, and the journey through it, a wonderful adventure. On the way we crossed the Thar Desert, and parts of the Aravalli mountain range where my uncle, a geologist, had discovered traces of uranium.

Jodhpur was an intense experience. One could feel its life pulsating at every corner. The world came alive for me in the everyday living drama of people and things. In the street outside the three-story *manzil* (small high-rise) where my *masi* (mother's sister) lived, the crows cawed, the kids ran around barefoot with runny noses, and the poor went about begging, and some child or the other would be crouched under the four-foot tap having a bath. Shopkeepers sat cross-legged behind heaps of food, fanning themselves, continuously shooing flies away from their sweetmeats, except when they became engrossed with a customer, talking animatedly, and the flies swarmed back to sit on the bright-orange syrupy *jalebis*. The street smelled of greasy but tempting snacks, strong *ittar*, perspiration, cow dung, and, when you passed a walled corner, urine—which would have shared the same space as the red spit of *paan*. Popular songs blared unbearably loud on the radios, the *rickshawalas* yelled for people to get out of their way as they cycled, half-standing on their pedals in an attempt to maintain balance with their heavy load of school kids. The *sabji-walas* too called out, displayed their wares, forcing four different varieties of squash on hurrying passersby. *Tongas* clattered on the uneven stones to the mesmerizing clip-clop of horses' hooves. Dogs copulated. And the squabbling, the haggling, the banter of everyday life. All this was intoxicating, but I was happy simply to walk through it, an unparticipating passerby.

We did not have the good fortune of knowing all our grand-parents, and *Nana,* Ma's father, who was known as Chotmal Sa Anchalia, was the only one left. He lived with Ma's youngest brother, but was very old and spoke only Marwari, which Raj and I couldn't follow at all. Walking bent over on a cane, he hardly ever spoke anyway, and when he did, his words were unclear because he had no teeth. I always thought he had blue eyes, but the color was really the glaze of old age. Until a little after India's independ-ence, he ran a bus service from Jodhpur to Peshawar, but when the bus industry was nationalized, he lost his business and had to start all over again, repairing buses instead.

Ma was very close to her younger brother and he was probably her confidant in all things. They could talk together for hours. Ever since I could remember, he would place his hand on my head, throw back his head with a laugh and say, "*Ye bechari bohot hi bholi hai*" (This poor thing is far too naive). *Paan* was always tucked in the side of his mouth, and the inside of his lips were always stained red. He had a knack for using analogies and speak-ing in proverbs, which I found fascinating. He would say, "Even a snake has to straighten himself out to get inside his home," or, "Like putting henna on your hands, to start anything, one must start at the heart of it."

We had many relatives in Jodhpur, and we would split our stay between them. Mostly though, we stayed with our paternal uncle, an eminent lawyer, and his family of eight children. His house was in the middle of the *chowk* (downtown intersection). Our family was given the third floor. Climbing the stairs to our quarters was difficult because each stone step was about two feet high and uneven from wear. Most nights we slept on the terrace where the air was cooler. I loved to be in the open, on a bed made of hard rope and a light mattress.

Raj had an unending enthusiasm for mechanics; and he would be totally enthused when the monsoons drenched the city, watching from the window of our uncle's house as the cars tried to negotiate their way in deep water, most times getting stuck on the pot-holed surface.

What I found truly captivating in Jodhpur were the five-kilometer fort on the hill and the marble temple, the *Thada*, on the smaller hill next to it. They are known as the Mehrangarh Fort and the Jaswant Thada, but to my child's mind the names were insignificant. We visited both places every time we went to Jodhpur. The long hard climb up to the fort was too strenuous for Ma and Baba, so it was just the younger ones who made the day trip. It would take us half a day to go through the massive gates up to the top of the fort. The open passages were about ten feet wide, and high stone structures enclosed them as they wound their way around the side of the hill. Above the walls, at intersections, were small rooms with pretty, arched windows, from which I imagined old-time sentries and king's aides leaning out to have a look at who was approaching.

To reach the top of the fort was exhilarating. All the buildings were constructed of large pink stones so that the houses could remain cool in the summer months. Standing next to the immovable cannon at the top of the fort, we would view the tiny houses through the shimmering haze of warm air. I could see the desert roll into the periphery of the city, but I could not see the beautiful *tilas*, the sand dunes. In later years, when I visited Jodhpur, I would think of how these *tilas* represented the brevity and granularity of life, so easily destroyed and recreated with every scorching gust of wind. How many times, visiting the picnic spots outside the beautiful city, had I etched my name on the sand, and how many times had it scattered my identity into nowhere.

At the heart of the fort were the royal suites, which had an ancient charm. It was to these chambers that the royal women and children retreated whenever the bugle sounded for war. The heavy brocade of the furniture and the curtains, and the intricately gilded cradles would set my imagination wild with stories of courage and heroism. I had heard that a long underground tunnel ran between the fort and the home of the royalty, Umaid Bhawan, a palace on the other side of the city. It was used for escape. Visiting the fort often made me wonder whether it would be worth living beautifully but in captivity. Now I know undoubtedly that it is better to be free at all costs.

It was in Jodhpur, when I was around thirteen, that I had my first fleeting experience of being the object of hidden male desires.

We were visiting a relative's house one evening. As we finished our meal and started to disperse into the hallway, one of my older, more notorious relatives got hold of me. At the time I did not know about his reputation, but much later in life one of my cousins mentioned his womanizing ways. He spun me around as I left the room, and in the dark corridor, body against mine, squeezed my behind. He released me as quickly as he had grabbed me. Later when his stare bore into me, I pretended nothing had happened. Let him try again, I thought, and I'll march straight to his wife and tell her. His wife was gorgeous and I admired her— he really had no need to look elsewhere. But pity soon took the place of anger as I thought of how the knowledge would cause her pain. How could I tell her and keep peace with myself?

Another of my relatives would follow me upstairs after lunch, while the others were having their naps, or at night, when we were preparing for bed. I was too naive to understand the full extent of his intentions initially, and nothing ever came of it until one afternoon. But then I managed to extricate myself from his room as he got the better of me. He had managed to wrestle more than a kiss, and his hands had groped almost every private part of my body.

I never told my parents or anyone else about these encounters. I assumed these things just happened, that they were part of life, in much the same way as a scolding, or a fall, or an unwanted intrusion. The world seemed full of oddities. It seemed that in this suppressed society, with an ancient civilization and lofty ideals, breaking of rules was frequent. And I understood that in the vast subcontinent of India, all kinds of behavior were able to coexist, such was the unspoken and strange forbearance of the people there.

The Teen Years

As much as I loved my summers in India, I was unprepared when my parents decided that both Raj and I should go to boarding school there. They wanted us to receive a "know-your-heritage" education. Resistant at first, I was finally packed off to SKV Gwalior, an old, ex-British school in Central India. Raj was sent to the very prestigious Mayo School in Rajasthan.

The boarding school was everything I had read about in books, and I soon warmed to the new environment. It was there I learnt to write Hindi, the basics of which Ma had taught us. For the first time I learned Sanskrit prayers, which conveyed for me an enormity—a vast sacredness and sanctity that conjured deep feelings of another realm, another reality, another universe, that was far more beautiful than the world I lived in. It was a place where decency, integrity, and loyalty flourished, and where the gods prevailed.

I stayed at the boarding school for three months, and when I came home for my holidays, I couldn't make myself go back. Raj had not lasted even a month at his school.

If my parents had wanted to protect us from Western influences, they certainly did not realize that India was fertile ground for all kinds of contradictory activities. Western influences were slowly creeping into Indian culture, not only disturbing the surface but coexisting. The thought patterns of the Indian mind tried to manage both—living by Indian traditions and acting under Western influences.

Although I had only been at the boarding school in India for a short time, the experience had seriously changed my outlook, and I did not return to my old routine. I strongly identified with the philosophical, artistic, and spiritual aspects of the culture, and they subdued me in spite of the boisterousness of the days I had spent there. I became a little wiser and was able to apply some level of free intelligence to cultural decisions. My parents had triumphed in their objective to Indianize me.

Now I would often spend time at the International School of Bangkok by myself. It was not that I could not make or keep friends, but that the environment disturbed my feelings and thoughts. Even when boys would ask me out, I told them I was not allowed to date, though I had never actually asked Ma if I could. I simply assumed that my parents would not have approved.

As time went on I found myself withdrawing more and more. There was a gap between life at school and that at home. There was a meaningless absurdity in this divergence that would need to be unburdened in later years. Pressured by two cultures, subscribing fully to neither one, I indulged in my own world of silent experiences.

One of the most memorable experiences of my life came when I was sixteen, when my father presented me inadvertently with a most precious gift: a spiritual journey to Kashmir. Although Baba did not advise me or even discuss everyday issues with me, he was a role model for that part of me which I will term sublime. He had always been an intrinsic inspiration for me. Growing up, I had watched him and learned that one could reach one's goals through planning and hard work. He was a small-town boy who had achieved international success. He wrote several books while he worked for the United Nations and when he retired he became the vice-chancellor of Jodhpur University in India. He believed that no matter how high one's status, having humility was an even higher, nobler state of being. I wish I had told him more often how proud I was of him. But ours was mostly a silent relationship of understanding.

Baba took Raj, Ma and me to visit the Amarnath caves, a holy sanctuary in Kashmir situated at a height of about seventeen thousand feet. It was in that distant unending vastness of the mountains that I truly felt God's existence. Down in the valley, in a place called Pahalgam, we started our journey. A beautiful narrow river of pure, cool water ran along the scattered rocks there. The early morning mist unveiled this hidden treasure in a slow dance as we started our ascent. Thick, birchlike forests exuded their woody scent, birds chirped, the clip-clop of our horses' hooves caused the scurrying of small creatures. The sacredness of the actual point of homage could be felt far below, in this deep gorge. For me, this was the wooded retreat I had longed for since childhood. Nature was brimming to the full. As artists we sketch its greatness, but our world is so vastly supreme that what little we capture as art is of no consequence, except as a tribute.

It was a three-day pilgrimage on horseback and we traveled with four guides. We climbed high into the mountains, now trekking, now on horseback. The sun was hot and the warmth seeped into our veins. Skins peeled easily at those heights and I could feel the burn on my face already. The first night was spent on the shore of Sheshnag Lake. We slept in small cots of coarse rope in an open shelter: no walls, just a roof. There was no doubt about its safety, for the purity of the revered site permeated every material element. The early morning sky enhanced the transparency of Sheshnag Lake, and the wide body of milky aqua nestling in the midst of the snowy mountain peaks seemed unearthly. In the presence of this sanctity, I breathed deep of its divinity and form, deliberately etching it into my mind so intensely that nothing should ever erase it. I was inside one of life's most profound and treasured moments, stored in the back of the mind and cherished, slowly, when the soul needed food for life. The miracle of that world cannot be brought into civilization, for nothing in the material world can retain the impact of that perfection.

The second day we experienced snowfall and were ushered into a tent that was offered to us by some kind men who provided us with a hot meal of oil-soaked *parathas* (Indian bread) and thick *toor daal,* (lentils) and a corner to sleep. We started again early the next morning. It was dark. Thick black clouds in an overcast sky. I could not tell when night ended and daybreak ascended. We decided to take the shorter but far more risky route on this treacherous climb high up in the mountains, across massive boulders. There was just enough time to reach our destination and return if we took that shortcut, because of the weather. The footholds of the horses were insecure and they would slip from time to time on the uneven slippery terrain created by the warmed glaciers that connected the mountains.

And finally we were there, facing the mouth of the cave. Inside was the ice formation of Lord Shiva, a crystallized, unchiselled column of frozen water reaching down from an opening in the roof, growing bigger as it descended, until it touched the floor. Pilgrims had offered petals to the Lord, having scattered them with love and devotion at the base of the symbolic altar. There were very few other people around: this was the dangerous monsoon season. Even though encumbered with a family, Baba had wanted to brave this pilgrimage.

This was my first exposure to what men and women called god, the omnipresent life-force. It was the best gift my father gave me.

The war in Vietnam was on. The economy in Bangkok was soon booming, with American soldiers around. For many local women it suddenly became easy to make extra money. As I retreated increasingly into myself, I thought: there are no laburnums here to make people happy, only tiny little green leaves that cover the murky gray water in the klongs. My male schoolmates began receiving letters informing them that they were being drafted into the army.

Inspiration came to me not from the world around but from within —from fantasies of nature, expressed through some form of art. I indulged in Emerson and Thoreau, and spent many languid hours at my desk, late into the night, reading Omar Khayyam, Tagore, and Khalil Gibran, or staring out at the *klong* and the blinking lights. I was the child on the shore picking white pebbles. I was the shy young bride with scented flowers in my hair. I tasted sweet words. I clung to ephemeral thoughts, each whisked quickly away by an equally wistful one. But really, they were as distant from me as I was from myself. I thirsted for natural beauty, for the deep woods and the purple flora under the great green fern. I wanted to smell the moss and touch its softness; I engrossed myself in Byron and Shelley. Some kind of sadness or melancholy was enveloping me, connected to the struggle between real living and life's romantic longings. It has taken me decades to reconcile the two. My private world was so different from the one I inhabited with friends and family; how was it that the rest of the world was concerned only with daily strife?

Contributing to my languor and melancholy was the fact that no one was pressuring me about the future. I had a brilliant sister who was studying physics, and my parents' ambitions were focused upon her. And there was the sole male child as well. I was the middle one, and they pretty much left me to my own devices. All they wanted was that I go to college, get married, and have babies. I was to have an average, happy life. And that is how I came to go to the University of Delhi, while my brother was sent to Columbia and Stanford in the United States. In the end, it turned out that my parents were not as broad minded as they appeared to be, and they followed the traditions of India, lavishing their hard-earned income on their only male child.

Two

Coming of Age

ORDEAL BY FIRE

The University of Delhi: Freedom and First Love

The university campus was in the old, historic part of Delhi, very far from the well-planned streets of the newer suburbs. The campus was not large, especially by North American standards. There was, however, a vast area behind that was a tamed landscape of beautiful trees. The yellow two-storey residence where I lived was on the left of the compound and housed about two hundred young women. Across from the large iron gates of the campus was a place where loafers would hang out, smoking their cheap brands while waiting for their luck with a passing *behenji* (miss). There was a bus stop and a mailbox, and next to these sat vendors roasting sweet corn on their tiny *chulas* (charcoal stoves), almost burning the kernels, just the way I liked. You had to devour the corn with lots of red chili, salt, and lemon to retain the taste in the mouth long after the demise of the corn seeds.

I met Nandita on my first day there, as I walked into the empty hallway of the hostel. We had both arrived a couple of days ahead of schedule and seemed to be the only ones scouting around, our cotton bags dangling from our shoulders. She saw me first. I still remember the way she walked straight toward me, her head tilted to one side, grinning from ear to ear.

"What sign are you?" she asked boldly.

"Leo," I answered, understanding her question immediately. "What's yours?"

"Leo!" she exclaimed in delight.

She had large beautiful eyes and light, shoulder-length hair, and I was instantly drawn to her impish charm. We decided to room together—two Leos with almost the same birth date and similar personalities. How rowdy we could get in a crowd, and be dead serious when there were just the two of us, alone. Before long, we were the ring leaders of our group. We chose a room on

31

the main floor, right in the middle of the hustle-bustle—next to the mess and near the laundry, in the center of everything, like the policed roundabouts prevalent on the roads in India. We were in touch with all the goings-on. We made friends with the *dhobiwala* (washerman), the *istriwalla* (ironing man), and the lady in charge of the mess. Even the senior girls warmed up to us, and that kept us fairly protected from excessive ragging. There was a hostel warden—a strict Bengali spinster—whom none of us wanted to displease, because we needed favors from time to time, when we had people visiting. In time, we chose a third roommate, a more subdued girl who complemented our wildness nicely. Looking back, I think we also took Mridula in because we were sure that she would win the Miss College beauty contest. Of course she did.

I was studying psychology and philosophy, both requiring memorization, a skill I did not possess. Indian students were taught by rote from the beginning, so I was no competition for them. But psychology was a passion and I breezed through it. People intrigued me with their diverse natures and beliefs, what drove them as they were tossed about by circumstances. What shaped a person? What experiences does one remember, and why only those? Can one *really* know anyone else? I believed I could understand only artists, poets, philosophers, for they were the only ones who revealed their true natures.

Nan, who was half Bengali and half Assamese, also studied philosophy. She would come back from class and challenge me, asking: "Buddha says the world is changing all the time, so tell me, why can't we see it changing?" Discussions were serious business. We argued and bantered. I teased her about her faults, and she did likewise with me. I told her she was bossy and incorrigible, and could analyze herself to death. She said my moods changed too often and I never did the dishes; and I had a very crude sense of humor (which I knew to be true, and this was our only point of agreement). She told me about her school crushes, about the pilot whom she hoped to marry one day, and later, about the handsome debauchee who was vigorously pursuing her. I told her again and again that I didn't care to whom my body belonged, it was a soul I needed! It was part of my heroic cynicism—did it come from the mystic Meera who was married but gave her heart to Krishna? We both had the call of the wild in our hearts, and yet, in spite of our rowdy extrovertedness, we shared an intense belief in the spiritual life and its mystical callings. I developed a relationship with her that I had longed for all my life.

For us, university was a time of self-discovery. There was a Hanuman temple by the river near the campus that Nan and I regularly visited. We would buy the dry, granular *besan-ke-laddoo* (a sweet) on the way to the temple as an offering. We often saw an old woman sitting on the steps of the temple, eating an evening meal consisting of a dry roti, a small pungent-looking onion, green chillies, and salt. Sometimes we would bring her a *laddoo*. For a few weeks, Nan and I thought that we could live on her diet, that the asceticism would make our minds and spirits strong, but alas, we never actually lived our lofty philosophies. Further north of the college campus, there were several Tibetan *dhabas*, their tents full of students clamoring for hot chow mein. We had several meals there before we learnt that the food contained dog meat.

There were long solitary walks in the luscious green grounds, where going barefoot in the early morning dew would make my heart and body tender for what I believed were defects in God's world. I thought too much about the plights of others. Yoga was at 6:30 a.m.

In India I found that I had easy access to those things that I had been intrinsically craving to learn but had been unavailable to me. When I asked the university authorities about sitar lessons, I was told that they could arrange for a sitar master to come, but I would have to pick him up from the bus stop because he was blind. So every Monday morning at six o'clock I would go outside the gates where the Masterji would be waiting for me, take him lightly by the elbow, and lead him on the very long walk to a classroom on the far side of the campus. When I spoke to him I wondered if he could hear the pity in my voice. Afraid to hurt his pride, I tried not to show him what I felt. In spite of what I considered to be his handicap, he showed me how to change the sitar strings, and how to hold its frets. And patiently he taught me how to play beautiful ragas on the four-foot instrument. He taught me the many techniques of playing, including *meed* and *gamak*, *jhala* and *taal*. And he taught me compassion. When he was a small child, he told me, his mother had put the wrong drops in his eyes and he had been blinded. Her one minute of blindness caused a lifetime of blindness in her son. How cruel his fate had been. Who had suffered more from this calamity, he or his mother? But he had reconciled himself to his destiny a lifetime ago and had poured his energy into transforming himself. He was biased towards me, and so he quickly had me teaching the more junior players. One day, three years after we began our lessons together, he came to my hostel in a three-wheeler auto, instead of the bus, and presented me with a sitar. Proudly, he asked me to look at the carving on the string holders. Crafted in ivory, each head was exquisitely shaped like a minaret, the wood ascending in rounded coils until it reached a tiny ivory pinnacle. I was utterly moved; his generosity and kindheartedness brought tears to my eyes. I knew how much I owed him, not only for this sitar, but for the deep love of ragas he had imparted to me, and the sensitivity to blindness he had imprinted on my mind.

On my dreamy walks by the gates of the campus, I would pass a middle-aged woman selling glass bangles. Her skin was hard and leatherlike from sitting outside (and perhaps due to other travails), but she had a pleasant, inviting face, and an upbeat tone. She squatted cross-legged on the rough red ground, with hundreds of gorgeous glass bangles called *chudis* spread neatly in front of her. When the sun shone at just the right angle, they would reflect beams of colored light, their rays catching in my eyelashes. When I lifted them up to the sun, they would tinkle softly. I lingered in that ethereal world, my eyes arrested by the sunshine and glass, expecting my heart to fill with wonder as the woman whispered, "*Lelo, lelo, behenji*" (Take it, take it, Miss). I bought half a dozen once, thinking I could hold on to their dainty splendor.

Many evenings I would break out of my two-storey dorm through the only stairs that led to the rooftop. The terrace was a quiet, private place where no one else ventured. With pencil and paper, I would sketch frantically, racing to catch the moment before Nature flung a new expression into the fleeting skies. Or, imitating Tagore, I would scribble my thoughts down as they tumbled out of my head.

Those were good days, the young carefree years:

"…and the boys' will is the wind's will and the thoughts of youth are long, long thoughts" [Tennyson].

Nan and I had a good friend, Arti. She was a Hindu and was totally, madly in love with a Muslim boy. Consuming them, physically and emotionally, was an intimacy both reckless and passionate. If I have ever seen two people give themselves up completely to love and all its pain and ecstasies, it was Arti and Ahmed. Her soul waited in torment for Ahmed's every gesture of love, and although she knew he returned her love, she had an intense and relentless dread of losing him. Her soul was filled with such intensity that we thought she would go mad if he admitted he was not able to marry her. Yet the pressures of Indian society made a Hindu-Muslim marriage an enormous risk. She seemed to sense the possibility of impending doom and was tormented by the prospect of a fate she could not control. Many times we watched the teardrops running down her swollen cheeks as she sobbed uncontrollably, in excruciating agony. I had met Ahmed several times with Arti outside the college gates. He was tall and handsome, as she was fair and beautiful.

But alas, the norms of society would not release them from its historical clutches. Many months after I completed university, I heard that Arti had become paralyzed in her legs, having jumped off the balcony of her house in Hyderabad when Ahmed married a Muslim girl. Why did society have to impose its own imperfections on a perfect love? No, I thought then, better Romeo and Juliet's end than to live by half measures. It was human frailty, not strength, that settled for less.

It was in my first year of university that I met a young man, Rajesh, who became my first boyfriend. He was an engineering student, also studying in Delhi, and was handing out prizes at one of the many art competitions I entered. He was good looking, and attracted me with his gregarious, carefree manner and good humor. This was the first time I experienced the feeling of love. At first, he came a couple of times to meet me in the residence and we simply talked and laughed. But as we got to know each other, came the shy kisses and the delicious feeling of first love. We whiled away our time in discos and movies, or sitting on his motorbike in Connaught Place, which throbbed in those days with the pulse of Delhi life. I loved riding on that bike, the wind in my face and hair, alert to the thrill of every sharp turn. Months passed and there was no doubt that I was enjoying the attention I received and my new sense of freedom.

But Arti and Ahmed were fresh on my mind, and my passion could not match theirs. In my more sober moments, I knew this man could not to be my life partner. He was boisterous and perhaps a bit too flirtatious. He was not able to reach that deeper side of me, for it was an intensely emotional link I was yearning for. Still, I continued to see him. Finally, when Ma and Baba came to visit, I introduced him to them—I needed their approval of him, in any case. I told them that he came from a good family, and that he would not have come to see them if he was not serious about marriage. Carefully, not wishing to upset me, they advised me against the relationship, saying that they could find a more suitable match from our Rajasthani community. I yielded to their wisdom, relieved at the closure of something I had not been able to settle for myself.

Baba was not pleased with me—Indian girls were not supposed to have boyfriends before they got married. When he went back, he wrote to me in his tiny handwriting: "My fragrant flower, I never thought you would do this."

It was the first time I had truly disappointed him.

A Brutal Experience, A Bitter Lesson

Spring has arrived; how can the winter not warm up to her? I feel I am in the mood to roam. My heart aches for something I cannot grasp.

It is a crisp midmorning. The dew has vanished from the leaves, and I gulp the air in as deep as my lungs can take it. I walk along the path in a park close by the college. There are few other people about, but I am happy to be alone, it's soothing to be by myself, and I am glad I chose to wear these light orange cotton pants with matching top. My friend Malini loves that orange sari of mine and wanted to borrow it, and she lent me this outfit in return.

As I reach an area where the path turns rugged, to pass through a cluster of trees, two men in police uniforms suddenly step into my path. Startled, I take a sharp breath. There is something suspicious about their crumpled brown attire and the way they have made their appearance out of nowhere. They are both middle aged. The bigger one of them gestures me to come along with them. I try to ignore him, but something in their crude stare and the way they hold their batons tells me I will not have much choice.

I don't exactly panic, but I take a few hesitant steps back, trying very quickly to sum up the situation. But the second one, who looks more agile, takes a step toward me. Before I am really aware of it, they have tackled me to the ground. Pushing my face down onto the ground, littered with leaves and twigs, they warn me in harsh but not loud tones to keep my mouth shut. I am too alarmed to cry out or resist. They come down on me, one after the other. I can't feel anything, not even the pain, but I know the worst is happening. The weight, the hands, the baton. The shuffling feet. The leaves, the earth, the rough undergrowth. The hurt. The warnings keep coming. My mind is spinning, my limbs are pulp, and my senses cannot recover. And then, it is over. They have left. I lie there longer than I need to, collecting my scattered thoughts and the emotions I thought I had lost. I get up on weak legs, stumble. I start to run. Dashing through a barbed wire fence, which appeared from nowhere, I don't know whether the rip in the bottom of Malini's pants is greater than the fissure that is deepening in the crevices of my mind.

By the time I got back to the room, I was in full grasp of reality. Only Nan was there, thank God. I unburdened myself, not able to disclose all the details, as if holding back would make things disappear—as if by not bringing them to my tongue, they would be declared unreal. Nan helped me through the crisis that afternoon as I undressed. Very quickly I had come to believe that the best thing to do was dismiss the incident as best as I could. Still, disease and pregnancy worried me terribly. Nan and I never ventured on the subject again, but for a good month or so afterwards, she kept asking me if things were okay.

Thank God I wasn't pregnant.

I did not tell anyone else or write to my parents about the rape. The vulnerability to judgment was too great and I did not allow the incident itself to surface to the mind. I wanted to brush it off. But it was more difficult for me to come to terms with the loss of my innocence and the fact that I was no longer a virgin. And I knew there was nothing anyone could do about that. It was easier to suppress the ugly memory of an event, no matter how traumatic, than to fuss over it, giving it a larger-than-life importance. I have wondered, in the years since, how I was able to survive the mental trauma. Perhaps I survived the ordeal because it never really touched my inner life, my true world. Now I do not even remember where the park was, or how I got back to the room, or in what month the incident happened.

But the brutal violation did finally take its toll on me, in a way

I never imagined, through the effect it had on someone else—the man I married.

The End of University

Summer came and it was wonderful to go home, to be in familiar territory and family surroundings, especially with Raj there. But before long July came, and I was heading back to the university, looking forward to seeing Nan, rooming with her again.

When I arrived, I went looking for her in the hostel but could not find her. I spotted her later near the classrooms. She saw me, and walking up to me, she said quietly, "Rita, my father committed suicide."

Clearly devastated, Nan told me the terrible story. She had returned home to discover her father's body hanging from the ceiling fan in the main bedroom. She had been alone at home at the time and had to bear the burden of grief by herself. I shuddered with disbelief. It was not the loss alone but the manner in which it happened that must have pierced her heart. She said that suicides were a curse in her family, many male relatives of hers had committed suicide.

Nan could not live at the hostel anymore, because she needed to rush home to be with her family. I saw Nan less and less. She tried to deal with her sad world, and the intimacy of our times together and the tumultuous friendship we had shared began to fade into a loving memory.

I began to channel my energies into the study of psychology and the lab work which I enjoyed so much. I worked hard for Mrs Kapoor, my psychology professor, who inspired me greatly. Her belief in me only encouraged me further to excel. It seems to me now that at every stage of life I have had my heroes, individuals who have inspired me. They helped make my own courage later seem effortless, as if I were merely acting in a mirror.

I still ached for Nan's companionship and could not replace her friendship. There were no young men in my life, by choice and by circumstance, and I retreated once again into myself. I was trying to make sense of the world, and failing in that pursuit, I created a distance from reality. I turned to writing poetry again. There seemed to be no sense in the workings of the varied world.

That summer Didi came to my rescue. When I got to Bangkok, she became enthused about having a two-woman art exhibition. She also enjoyed painting and we created one oil painting after another. My favorite was a portrait I made of a young girl, her face pensive, in shades of purple, burgundy, and gray. I called it *Reflection.* Ma's favorite was called *Barefoot in the Park,* a green and white semi-abstract of a woman, in shades that matched the underside of a Russian olive-tree leaf. She kept it in her bedroom. The exhibition brought me the same joy I had felt as a young teenager at my parents' cocktail parties. The experience was heady and flattering and it left a pleasant imprint on my mind.

My years at university were well-rounded and fulfilling. I participated in art competitions, wrote articles for the college magazine, debated world health issues, and taught sitar. I came to have a deep appreciation for India and Indians.

These university years came to an end at the same time as my family's tenure in Thailand, and Raj's completion of high school. My father was given the choice of one of several postings: Trinidad and Tobago, Libya, or any other developing nation that needed manpower planning. Ma and Baba chose Ghana, West Africa.

Three

The Suitable Match

Ghana: Listless Days and Looking for a Husband

In Accra, the capital of Ghana, we lived in one of four duplex apartment complexes on top of a small hill, the other three being occupied by other Indian and Chinese families. The suburb was sparsely populated. Most of the vegetation nearby was shrubbery, and in the distance were receding hills and pockets of greenery. I enjoyed the landscape—it was open to the elements and there was usually a pleasant breeze. It never got too hot in Accra, and the rains were nothing like the monsoons in the Far East.

Ramu was not with us now, we children having grown up. He and Ratna went back to India, to live in Allahabad. Ma did all the cooking, and I learnt to cook basics like *parathas, rotis,* and *aloo gobhi.* I had never seen Ma work in the kitchen before, but she was a wonderful cook and made many dishes in the Rajasthani style. When we had parties, she fried what seemed like hundreds of exactly the same size *puris.* I was amazed she could still do that! Baba drove himself to work in the city. We did not have a driver any more, and we did not need a gardener because we lived on the second floor.

Ghana used to be known as Gold Coast. The Europeans had long ago come here to profit from the gold and ivory. Ivory Coast was one of the adjoining countries. Ghana had also been one terminus of the thriving Atlantic slave trade. We visited Elmina Castle and other forts on the shoreline, where captured Africans from the interior were kept to await the slave ships. Abandoned and forlorn now, how busy and full of terror and tragedy they must have been back then. I cringed at the crashing of the waves, which threw their weight on the wide banks below the wooden structures at Elmina Castle, and fought the images that flashed in my mind. Nevertheless, I now realize that I was too young, naïve, and insulated to fully appreciate Africa, its cultures, and its history.

Accra boasted a small Indian community, mainly of established businessmen who sold clothes, spices, gems, and other Indian exports. Most of them had been living there for years and they were wealthy and respected citizens. It was not often that these businessmen and the UN personnel got together, but there was great cordiality between them whenever they did.

For most of the personnel in the diplomatic service, socializing consisted of gathering in the evenings at the Indian Embassy grounds to form a club of sorts. There couldn't have been more than thirty people, most of them older than me. There was badminton every night. The bougainvillea hung low over the yellowed walls of the Embassy compound; and the warm humid air was punctuated intermittently with wafts of a welcome breeze. These relaxed evenings were a time when people let go their masks and basked in the glow of their own aura and individuality. On Friday nights, when the Embassy ran an old Indian movie, the open-air compound would come alive, with an unburdened nonchalance. A light chatter suffused the air against the loud background chirping of the crickets. The short-lived glow of the fireflies fascinated me, and that vision served my want of an isolated experience in a remote corner when I needed to unburden my mind, as I often did.

I was free now, from academic work, and during the daytime I shopped with Ma or read. My brother's love for music sustained a part of our quiet lifestyle. Together we listened to music in every language. Understanding only a fraction of the familiar sounding words, we developed a lifelong fondness for Bengali drama, Marathi bhajans made well known by many of Maharashtra's classical singers, upbeat Rajasthani folk songs, and Urdu ghazals that conveyed very subtly the deep philosophies of love and life. We also enjoyed the terribly ancient songs which were sung "playback" in the black-and-white films. It was Raj's open-mindedness that influenced my appreciation for this diversity of music.

There were no girls close to my age in our small social circle.

But there were some boisterous young children who would come to the Embassy and who became close to me. There were six or seven of them, and they would be waiting for me. They would listen in awed silence to my stories of jungle adventures or space travel. I loved children but was in no hurry to get married. I would take my time.

But fate was making its own plans for me.

In India, young women just finishing university are considered ripe for marriage. It is a preoccupation of all mothers to find suitable sons-in-law for their daughters as soon as they seem to be blossoming into womanhood. Arranged marriages were still the norm, and I did not have any objections to them—they had come a long way since the days of my parents. We were allowed to meet our prospective spouses, spend time with them, interview them to our hearts' content. There was no guarantee, in any case, whether an arranged marriage or a "love" marriage would stand the test of time.

Needless to say, my parents were already hunting around for eligible bachelors. But their search was only halfhearted. It was an impossible task, they claimed, considering where we were. In a place thousands of miles from home, how could they possibly find me a husband?

Among the older generation who frequented the Embassy gatherings, there was one couple in particular, the Nayars, who became very dear to me. They were from Kerala, a state in the southern tip of India where the customs were very much in contrast to those of Rajasthan, where my family came from.

I had a deep respect for Mrs Nayar's simple way of life and her religious fervor. She seemed to fit exactly the image of a dutiful wife, who in my mind's eye was draped in a beautiful creamy silk sari with a large red border. Mrs Nayar was an ounce of gold, but a little too worried about the well-being of her family of two boys and a dear husband. She was fierce in her admiration and love of her husband, a self-made man, a spiritual seeker, a Vedantic scholar. He looked the part. His very distinguished and well-chiseled features and his stoic mannerism seemed to be touched by a faint air of arrogance, though I felt then that he was more than entitled to it. He had made something great of himself from the deprived youngest child of a poor family of seven children. Mr Nayar, like Baba, had also worked his way up to join the UNDP as a statistician and an economist. His life had been a harder struggle than Baba's.

They told me their elder son would soon be coming home for his summer vacation.

At the same time, Ma and Baba found a traditional Rajasthani but brilliant PhD candidate (very sought after by other parents), whom they asked me, for the hundredth time, to reconsider. They insisted simply from lack of choice. But I had no intention of settling for the only person they could find. I needed more choice. I knew that my parents were more preoccupied with settling into their new life. Also, sending Raj abroad to study seemed a more urgent priority for them than my future. I decided therefore that finding my own match would be better than sitting at home and indefinitely waiting for my parents to come up with something.

Find my own match, I did. And the cruel destiny that came along with him.

The Suitable Match

I met Shan in June of the same year that I arrived in Ghana. He was broad shouldered, not much taller than I, and looked very academic in his rectangular glasses with dark frames. He had a head of thick wavy hair, and his fair complexion was a shade lighter than mine. He was home from the University of Sheffield for his summer holidays. At first I would meet him briefly at the Embassy club, where he had been coming for a few days, and we would exchange polite hellos. Then one day I broke the ice.

He was wearing light-colored pants and a dark blue half-sleeved shirt. We were standing next to the badminton court, with

Raj and his young friends.

"Your mother had told me you were coming," I said, racket in hand. "Do you play?" He confessed modestly to playing for the college league. We talked briefly then about university. He was studying chemical engineering and was in his second year.

The next day he came in his white gear. He had a racket, the strings of which he was testing, bouncing them against his wrist.

All those playing badminton took turns, since there was only one court. When we were free, Shan and I got together to chat.

"What do you do with all the time on your hands?" he asked me. His arms were crossed, as we stood beside the court, watching a game in progress.

He looked very relaxed.

"Nothing much. I'm awaiting my results. Then I'll think about what to do," I replied vaguely. I really did not know how I was going to spend the next little while.

We played badminton every evening. There was little else to do. Over the course of the next few weeks, a friendship began between Shan and me, built upon mutual respect. He was well-mannered and preferred more to listen than to talk. The meetings were always with other people around, and we would enjoy the relaxed, inconsequential conversations between the games and the occasional soda.

When we played badminton, I usually ended up playing doubles against him.

"Stop aiming your shots at me!" I would yell to him on the court. That was his way of teasing me and discreetly flirting.

He would come over to our house, apparently to visit Raj, who was a few years younger than Shan. But I think he really came to meet me. He would stay just long enough, and keep the appropriate distance between us. He was courting without trying to make it obvious. I respected Shan and felt flattered by his attention. He did not ask me out, as there was really no place to hang around, but I visited his home a couple of times and helped his mother with gardening or shopping.

About a month after our first meeting, while we were standing on the steps of the porch of the Embassy, he said quite unexpectedly, "I have a girlfriend, you know." His grin appeared wide in his square jawline. It was a feature that fascinated me, that I may have wanted my children to inherit.

The hubbub of the evening was fading and people were starting to leave the grounds, saying their good nights and making their *namaskars* (greetings).

"Oh yeah?" I asked with a smile. "Is she in England—is she at university with you?"

"No, she's in Tanzania. I met her in high school." I knew that his father had been stationed there for five years before they came to Ghana. Shan had been sent to England to do his A Levels while his father had been posted in Dar es Salaam.

"What's her name?" I challenged.

This was unexpected personal conversation, though not unwelcome.

"Radha," he said softly. His shy and cautious nature prevented him from saying more. He had wanted to share this information with me and I was flattered. I would discover his intent soon enough.

"So how do you see each other? How come she's there and you're in England?"

A minute elapsed.

"We'll work something out," he said, looking straight ahead into nowhere. Shan looked uncomfortable and probably felt awkward about having revealed too much of himself. Yet it seemed he needed to have this conversation.

"What about you? Don't you have someone?" he inquired with a sideways glance.

"No, not any more. I met someone at university but things didn't work out."

"Oh?" This was not concern but genuine interest—a purposeful curiosity. "What happened?"

"My parents didn't want me to marry him—they thought it wasn't a good match," I said, looking away. The truth was that I had not wanted to marry Rajesh. I was not sure why I now wanted to hide the truth from Shan. Was it because I feared he might think I was incapable of love? Little did he know! I liked Shan but I had not quite thought over the nature of my interest in him. Now of course there was this Radha.

One warm morning, I drove into town to buy groceries with Ma. I had promised her that I would make sandwich rolls for the party the next day. Having bought the essentials at the Kingsway grocery store, we proceeded to walk the short distance to the crowded and noisy open-air market. I enjoyed shopping there. Carts were piled high with corn, yam, potatoes, and multitude of other produce. Ma and I jostled through the crowds, going from stall to stall, picking and choosing, haggling and shouting. When I looked up at the end of it all, bags in hand, I spotted Shan several meters away. He was too far to converse with, but we saw each other. He seemed to be standing still, quite out of place, partly hidden behind other shoppers. He left unobtrusively. I wondered what had brought him here to the market. For a brief moment I imagined he had been spying on me; I dismissed the thought.

A few days later, Shan came to our home. He would be leaving for England in a couple of weeks. We sat in the room that was used as a study, where Raj would often laze about, lying upon a low *deewan*, (couch) listening to all sorts of music on tape. Shan sat down on the carpet in front of me, and coming close, facing me with what must have taken tremendous courage for such a shy, introverted person, he declared in his quiet way:

"I'd like to marry you. Would you—would you marry me?"

It took me just moments to understand the seriousness of his request. He had taken me completely by surprise.

My mind in a whirl, I blurted, "What about Radha, your girl-friend in Tanzania?"

"Don't you know, *you* are that Radha."

His confession was simple and I believed him instinctively. There was no reason not to.

Through my smile I told him I'd have to ask Ma and Baba. I needed their opinion, and I wanted time to think about his proposal.

I was inclined to accept him. His quiet manners were appealing and decency showed through his simple ways. He seemed not only serious and reliable, but also good natured and easygoing.

He would make a good husband, I thought.

My mother was supportive, even encouraging, of the idea of marriage into Shan's family. She was probably also relieved, having failed so far in finding me a suitable match. She even whispered in my ear that she thought he would make a good lover. Sometimes Ma surprised me. Was it his flushed cheeks when he played badminton, I wondered, that provoked her comment?

I had started falling in love. It was a very rational love, a love I was returning.

Within the narrow radius of my life's experiences, I had succumbed to the idea of marriage after a few weeks of trivial indulgence. The ebb and flow of life carried on its simple charade and lured me into its endless game. Shan fitted very well into the mould that most Indian girls have for a marriage partner: not bad looking; studying engineering in England with plans for completing his masters; same socioeconomic status; same religion. Although he was from a different part of India, and had a different mother tongue, he too had been partially brought up outside the country. I had met no one who commanded as much love and respect from me as his parents. I had heard incredible stories about problems that girls had with in-laws. I was utterly convinced that such good souls, with their dignity and calm, would not cause me the slightest heartache. They liked me for myself. Logic spoke for Shan as a good husband, even as my heart stood on the brink of love.

But I learnt from Shan that his father was vehemently opposed to our union.

"You cannot be serious about something like this at your age," his father had said. "You are twenty-two! You have to concentrate on your studies and forget about all this. This is a time to work hard to build your future, not think of marriage!" He also wanted a daughter-in-law from his own community to uphold the purity of lineage and tradition. Every Indian parent wished this then, and many continue to do so, of course.

Shan did not know how to react. He was distraught, and I knew that this would be a heavy decision for him. I prepared myself for any eventuality.

Shan's vacation ended and he returned to England for the start of his new term in August. We had not made any plans for the future, but I had a notion of what the possibilities might be. He wrote to me regularly and still seemed agitated at his father's opposition. It was hard for him to concentrate on his work, though in his letters he sounded quite determined that we would marry. But he could not figure out a way to win over his father.

At this juncture, I was unperturbed at the manner in which my life was unfolding, and the direction it might take. My passive nature made it easy for me to go with the flow, accept life as it was. So far it had been like a careless wave, bringing along a shiny pebble or two, but I had yet to see it bring forth its treasures. Perhaps they lay as deep as the ones in my own bosom, and perhaps they would remain there forever.

For Shan though, time dragged on. The wait and the indecision lay heavy on him. But Shan would have his opportunity that winter. When he came back to Ghana for his two-week winter break, he somehow managed to convince his father, who had little choice but to yield to the determination of his first-born.

My results from university had come and I was qualified to pursue a graduate degree. I had set my mind on studying either organizational development or mental testing and counseling, and since Shan was studying in England, I asked my parents for permission to join him. With a logic that was difficult to debate, they explained to me that I could indeed go, but I would need to get married first. No Indian parents would have sent their daughter off with a man, without first ensuring a permanent relationship. I consented to their request. It seemed that I had to plan my life without help; and I could do what I wanted as long as I stayed within the rules.

But there was no time for wedding arrangements then, and we decided to proceed with a quick, registered marriage, which would be followed by an elaborate family ceremony in the summer in India.

There was something on my mind. I did not tell Shan about my past, about the rape and the loss of my innocence. That had happened a few years ago and was behind me. I had accepted it as a twist of fate, and expected that anyone who married me for love would deem it an unfortunate part of my history. But in my heart I wanted to clear all accounts and I debated with myself many times how and when to tell him. It was not an easy thing to blurt out to anyone, let alone a man or a suitor. So I waited.

We signed the register in the tiny offices of the Accra city hall with both my parents and his mother present. His father did not come. The wide blue sheet that held our registration was neatly printed in little black handwriting, folded, and handed over to us.

Still living with my parents, I went to Shan's house for lunch that day. The place was hushed, not from household peace, but from the finality of a huge decision having been made through stubbornness alone. I will never forget that meal. Shan's father was ill-at-ease, choking on the simple food that had been served in the usual manner. He did not speak a word but left the table as unobtrusively as he had joined it. He offered me no greeting of any kind, yet he did not make me feel unwanted. It was a multitude of emotions within himself that he was trying to contend with. I understood him and felt sorry for the pain I had caused him.

There was nothing I could do or say, but I knew I had an infinite number of years in which to make up to him for the pain I had caused. I needed his blessings but I felt I was not entitled to them. Shan had got what he wanted, but I felt caught in between, the cause for someone's happiness and another's pain. I could have forgone the marriage for the sake of Shan's father, but in that case Shan would have been devastated. He loved me enough to have gone against his father's wishes.

After a few days, we flew to England. The marriage formalities had been so rushed and perfunctory that, except for the fact that I was going abroad, I felt nothing in my life had changed. But everything had changed, in a single day. The thought that the time to make the decision to marry is miniscule, compared to the years which will be spent in the marriage, makes one shudder.

Sheffield, the Days of Rage

It was January. And *it* started on the third day after our arrival in England. The daily torture of my husband's relentless rage. Looking back at those days now, I tremble to think how I bore four months of sheer hell, and instantly shrink from the prospect of that fate again.

I had come to England bringing with me bare essentials, mainly clothes. We had taken a train from London to Sheffield, about a three-hour journey, and when we arrived we had no choice but to live in Shan's single room at the coed dorm. The room must have been twelve by ten feet; it was extremely clean, with a single bed, a desk, a closet, and a small sink. Of course, living together was not permitted and we were on the lookout for a place, but it was next to impossible to find something in the middle of a school year. I could not eat at the mess and I did not have easy access to any facilities. I was not sure how we were going to manage but it didn't seem like an insurmountable challenge. We had just got married a few days ago, we would live on love.

The summer in Accra with Shan had been innocent, and we had not ventured into a physical relationship yet. Our final discovery of each other was a simple act, not particularly passionate and, it turns out, not memorable enough for me to recall the details. For someone who had awaited with anticipation the pivotal moment of ecstatic love making, the moment that came was one of disappointment. The act itself was expressionless, as if ownership and final opportunity were the motive. He was not absorbed in love but in the act of swift fulfillment. Instead of receiving intimacy, my body became subservient to his rational and dominating commands. Time did not stand still, and I waited in vain for emotional fulfillment.

On the evening of our third day of our new life in England, we were sitting on the hard blue carpet at the foot of the bed, chatting quietly and easily exchanging experiences, sharing information. We talked of our early years, and the experiences that had formed us. I was eager finally to get to know him better, to understand him and have myself understood. It felt good to be sitting there, slowly allowing ourselves to open up, discovering each other. Painful moments mingled with happier emotions. He was a good listener but volunteering information did not come naturally to his introverted nature—wife or no wife; love or no love.

I found myself doing most of the talking. Yes, I admitted, I suppose I had learnt to grow up alone and distant in the somewhat nomadic lifestyle of my family, and there were instances when I had liked so-and-so. No, I did not like to question my parents' practical wisdom. Yes, I was an artist by nature. I had won art competitions, that's how I had met that particular boyfriend. He was prompting me to talk, asking me discreetly, sympathetically, about the past. He had known about my previous dating, but now he wanted to know more. I chose to open up, eager to build a relationship of trust, honesty, and loyalty. In the deepening shadows of the evening, it was easier for me to fill in the blanks in his knowledge of me.

"Did you spend a lot of time together?"

"Whenever I was allowed out of the hostel, mostly during weekends... Yes, I suppose we did spend a lot of time together."

"Like Diana and me."

"Who's Diana?" I asked.

"My badminton partner here."

"Oh."

I had assumed that there had been no one except Radha, but I was happy to hear that I was not the only "guilty" party. His encouragement and the disclosure of his own experiences served its purpose. He was trying to make it easier for me to talk. I discovered much later that Diana had never existed.

We must have talked for quite a while. There were no distractions, there was nothing else vying for our attention. We had all the time in the world.

It had become dark outside. Light from the corridor through the gap under the door lit up the small corner where we sat. We were too absorbed in ourselves to turn our lights on. In fact, we had not moved at all for a while, he sitting on the floor at the foot of the bed, on my right.

It was then that I told him about the rape—the incident in the park, now almost three years ago. It took effort on my part—I could hardly get the words out. I had dismissed it from my mind, suppressed it, and artificially created its nonexistence. Now to revive it seemed almost a crime against myself. But I felt I had to share that hidden truth with my new life partner. Shan was eager to know the details, so I told him what had happened as best as I could.

If I had only had the barest hint of the extent of his treachery and the fury that was about to be unleashed on me, I would have shut up.

The questions came, one after the other, and rapidly.

"So tell me what happened, exactly."

"I was going for a walk."

"By yourself?"

"Yes, by myself…it was a crisp spring day…there were two men, in police uniforms…"

He quizzed me with a blank expression, leaning forward, his eyebrows raised ever so slightly, his manner urging me to continue. There was the faint sound of jazz playing on a radio somewhere. The light under the door gap went off, but I could still see Shan, faintly.

What exactly did you do? Why? How?

He was no more the concerned confidant. Instead, he declared an unspoken superiority and exerted his will.

I was uncomfortable now, but I continued. I wanted to surrender and move on.

I apologized for not having told him earlier.

In the stillness of the room, I could hear his breathing, slightly erratic.

And then it happened. With no warning, no hint.

Not even remotely had I anticipated what happened next. The assault.

His eyes are bulging as he clenches his teeth.

My head explodes from the force of his fist on the side of my head. He stands up, taking a step past me, turns around, and delivers an unrestrained kick to my stomach. I keel over from shock.

"How could you not tell me?" The tone flat and ugly, the voice low, deep, and cruel.

He is raging—but is clever enough not to yell too loud.

"Bitch! You should have told me!"

I cannot cry out. I have lost my breath. Life is being sucked out of me. I hug my stomach with both hands. My head is splitting, throbbing uncontrollably with every heartbeat. I lie on the ground, curl up and face down to avoid the punches that are still coming my way.

I hear him whisper coarsely in my ear that he will make me pay.

Survival

I could not move, not even turn my head to look at him. All I could feel was excruciating pain, in every part of my body. He had punched my arm, my face, whatever he could reach. Fear paralysed me, constricted my senses, my mind. After a while he stopped, went to the side of the bed, and sat down. I had not screamed, I was groaning. Perhaps I had been too afraid to scream.

Lying there on the floor, I searched for answers concerning my behavior. Being raped was certainly not my fault, but perhaps not having told him was wrong? Still, violence was unacceptable. I was angry. He had the option of leaving me, sending me back home, or yelling and screaming at me, but why physical cruelty? There was no history of violence in my family, and to me there was no excuse good enough for inflicting bodily harm on anybody. Whatever had happened in my past, I did not deserve that cruel reaction. How badly I had misjudged Shan, and how he had misled me about himself.

I lay on the carpet going over and over these thoughts, until sleep overtook my exhausted mind.

I woke up the next morning sore and aching all over. Shan was asleep on the bed—he had not changed or bothered to undress. I walked up to the sink, and saw a large swelling on my temple, above my left eye. The ache in my stomach made it hard to bend. I hoped there was no internal injury. My heart convulsed at the thought of what had happened last night.

I decided to try and remain calm and sort out the situation. Now that I had made my revelation and Shan had responded, perhaps we could go on with making our life together. I felt relieved at the thought. I could have phoned Ma and Baba and involved them in my problem, but they were too far to offer real help. The stupidity of having misjudged Shan's character also prevented me from calling them. They would have been sorely disappointed. Pride overtook self-preservation in the belief that I would be better served by apologizing to Shan.

When Shan woke up, I apologized. In my mind I knew it was only a halfhearted apology.

"I am really sorry. It was a mistake, I should have told you earlier," I said softly, looking down at him as he sat on the side of the bed.

"Mistake? Mistake! How can you dismiss this as a mistake? You tried to fool me!"

"I wasn't trying to fool you, I didn't get a chance to tell you."

"Well you should have—and now you'll just have to live with the consequences, won't you?" He looked alert now, his sleep all gone. "You'll have to pay for this."

I just wanted to make up.

"Please, I am really sorry."

"No—its not enough," he said, shaking his head. He got up, found his slippers, and started to leave the room.

"I need to use the washroom," I said.

"No, not now." He closed the door behind him. I heard the lock click.

And so his anger had not abated. He knew from my apologies that I was not going to get angry or fight back.

He was stubborn. I should have realized this when he defied his father. He was also impulsive and abrupt, as I had found out, and most of all, unpredictable. I remembered how sudden his proposal was, and how quickly everything had happened. And now he had beaten me almost senseless, when what I had needed was sympathy and understanding.

When he returned, he didn't say a word but changed his clothes quickly. Then he left without a word. He locked me in again before I could protest seriously.

I nursed my body with the help of the sink and whatever else I could use. In a way, I was glad he was away.

When Shan came back late afternoon, he let me use the washroom, guiding me to the door, keeping watch and waiting. He was probably afraid that I might report him to someone. But there was no one around in the corridor. I had no intention of telling anyone, in any case, believing that resolving our problem to his satisfaction was the only way to go on. He was still angry, I could tell, but more restrained.

Back in the room, I pleaded, wanting so badly to make up. "Please let's make up. I am so sorry about everything. I didn't realize you would feel this way, or I would have told you earlier."

He didn't reply. I tried to come close to him, become more intimate, where he sat on the bed, but he haughtily shunned me, in what he thought was his entitled supremacy.

Time passed, perhaps an hour. I didn't know what to do. He wouldn't accept anything I said and didn't offer any suggestions himself.

"Do you want me to leave? Shall I go back to Accra?"

There was nothing I wanted except to make up. I wasn't hungry or thirsty. I had drunk a bottle of leftover juice.

Still, he didn't reply. He lay on the bed, his arms crossed over his eyes, and fell asleep. This was going to be a pattern for the rest of our lives—this silent treatment. Shan's small round clock ticked away, minute by minute.

Finally I lay down on the floor to sleep.

In the middle of the night, he awoke.

"Get up!"

Slowly I sat up. He went and turned on the light.

"Papa was right. I should never have married you. He warned me that you had not been brought up in India, that you went to an American school. He said you may have easygoing morals."

"What has that to do with anything?" I retorted.

In a superior, unpleasant tone he began taunting.

"What else have you not told me? Is there anything else you haven't told me?" Brooding had driven him mad. "You'd better tell me now because if I find out later, you will really be in trouble," he said, leaning forward, shaking his head from side to side as if to say that I had better be afraid.

"There's nothing more to tell. I am truly, truly sorry. I shouldn't have caused you this pain."

"Tell me what else you've done!" He was working up a rage. Tell me *right now!*"

The blow came flying, landing on my lips and nose. Then another one on the arm, upon a bruise.

"Are you going to tell me? Bitch!"

This time I fought back. I hit him with whatever strength I could, pounding him with a fist. I was no match for his strength, however, and finally gave in, slumping down on the floor and crying. But he didn't care, repeating over and over how I had cheated him and how I would have to pay by suffering.

The next day he continued the same way. And the next, and the next. Locking me up, interrogating, harassing, and hitting me with his fists. There seemed to be no other outlet for his rage. My face had fast become unrecognizable: swollen cheeks, black eyes, cut lips. I did not defend myself. I couldn't. I should have fought back with every ounce of my strength. Instead, I felt powerless, defeated. Perhaps this is what he meant by, "You'll just have to suffer." He wanted total domination over me—physically and mentally. I recalled our courtship in Accra. I thought about the time I had seen him in the market—what had he been doing there, spying on me to see if I was with anyone? And what about the deviousness with which he had told me about his fictional girlfriend, Diana, just to get me to talk? He was manipulative and distrustful. And he had wanted me, whatever the cost to his family; not for love, but for possession.

A pattern was manifesting itself. I would apologize; he would refuse to accept my apology, responding in words that were spiteful and coarse, then the physical abuse would follow. Each time, I would surrender to a primitive fear. Fear of survival. There were no apologies from him, no attempts to make up during the quieter moments of the exhausting days and endless nights. For what may have been a week or two, I could hardly think as I drifted in and out of stupor, nursing my aching body. Bruises became a constant reminder of my new reality. I feared permanent damage to my tissues. Any wrong word or action would cause the already overwrought situation to deteriorate. I had no choice but to appease him when he was around, and when he wasn't, I shook, I froze, I threw up, I curled up. All my senses were focused on how I could survive yet another day.

I had thought about running away and going to the university authorities, but I feared that he would catch up with me and make the situation even worse. He was unpredictable and capable of hurting, maiming. Once when I had hit back, he had bit my ear. I also had a slight hope that he would come back to his senses and my trauma would end. It had to, sooner or later. I thought that enough apologies would one day pay off.

I had no access to money. I was living in the dorm illegally and did not want to face the residence authorities. I had no idea who else lived in the dorm. I did not even know the students in the next room. Shan supervised my every move and literally kept me locked up. The few times that he did not, I was too scared to run away. How far would I get in any case? He had brainwashed me— he would ruin me, destroy me. If I got out of line he would *deal* with me. He brought me food from somewhere, but my hunger was for compassion, not food.

We went to the drug store once. I needed ointment, cold packs, aspirin.

"I'll do all the talking," Shan instructed me as we went out.

Alert to his surroundings, he made sure I was by his side as we searched the aisles and paid the bill.

Once in a while he would get totally out of character and cry to himself, sometimes even saying under his breath, "I can't believe this is happening." During those times, he let me come close and he would hold me. "Don't ever do that again, don't ever lie to me, okay?" He would caress me. And then he would ask if there was anything else I wanted to tell him. Did he really expect me to tell him anything at all, even if I had something to tell?

It would be easier at such times in one's life if logic or courage could prevail. But fear had hurled me down into the depths of some endless void. Before the thought of escape could surface, it was quashed by the very same consciousness that conceived it. When someone has no reason for inflicting pain, then trying to deal with the situation through reasoning is futile. Love is blind, but then, so is hate.

Weeks turned into months. I cannot remember how I survived, day after day. Good days were when I got through without too many words or a fight. All I can remember now of those days is that it was a nightmare out of which there was no escape. The beatings decreased over time, coming impulsively, randomly, spurred on by a wrong word or action, or by his own thoughts feeding upon themselves.

One morning in late April or early May, we moved into a room off campus, in a house that belonged to a single lady. I can't remember her name now. Her manners were stiff and reserved. Perhaps, to give her credit, she had seen my bruises and did not want the burden of involvement.

I should have been ecstatic at the prospect of moving out, of living freely outside of the dorm, but my mind had become so numb by that time that it really did not matter where I was, or indeed if the world broke into two.

The first night in our new room, not yet unpacked, we slept on the floor. In the morning I woke up to see Shan fumbling around the boxes, looking for his toothbrush.

"Where'd you put my toothbrush?" he said, in a foul mood.

I helped him look. It was difficult to see in the dim light of the frosted bulb, but after some rummaging, we found his toothbrush.

"Wait till I get back," he said, wiggling his finger at me, his eyes bulging, his face knotted in a tight grimace and barely six inches from mine, "I'm going to take proper care of you."

There was menace in the flat tone and the hiss of his words. My heart froze at the thought of the disaster awaiting me. I felt the bile rise in my throat as I waited for him to leave.

For the first time, fear mobilized me. I grabbed both our passports from the small airline bag where I kept important documents and shot out of the room. With a calm face I asked the landlady whether she was going toward the university, and if so I could get a ride with her. Luck was on my side and she even went a little out of her way to drop me at the front door of the huge intimidating structure that was the main building. I headed straight for student services, still a little apprehensive but determined. There was a part of me that did not want the shame of exposure, for even freedom carries a fear of the unknown, but another part of me was urging me to move forward.

I was asked by the receptionist to sit in the waiting room. If the people there could have read my mind they would have seen fear, hope, relief, foreboding. Minutes went by, each nerve-wracking moment draining me of my strength and resolve. Everything around me seemed unreal. Where was I? What was I doing here? Would anybody help me? Or would they tell me it was not their problem? Would they ask *him* to join me and expect us to solve our own problem? Would they see my fear, my anxiety? What I feared most was that he would find me and drag me back like a dead carcass to the lion's den to finish me off once and for all.

A middle-aged matronly lady called Mrs Sharrock, whose face is etched in my memory for all time, came to talk to me. Hope flickered in me; more than hope. She understood my fear. And slowly as the story spilled out of me, and as she saw the visible signs of the abuse I had suffered, a look of concern enveloped her face. She took me to the medical center.

She would be back in the early afternoon, she told me, and take me home with her. At the center they treated me and must have given me sleeping tablets. I was thankful to be alone. I could finally breathe. The strength which had been sucked out of me during my months of emotional and physical torture slowly returned to my body. When I think of Mrs Sharrock now, I cannot help my emotion; I feel immensely thankful. I needed someone to take charge of me at that moment and she became my guardian angel. After contacting my parents in Ghana, she bought my train ticket from Sheffield to London. My father had sent back a telegram saying I should return home at once, an airline reservation had been made for me.

Although the immediate burden was lifted from my mind, I was still dazed. I listened as Mrs Sharrock explained the plans that had been made for me: a train ride to London that evening; a plane journey back to Ghana the next morning.

Mrs Sharrock left me at the train station. She must have been aware that I wanted to clutch on to her skirt like a child. Shan would have been searching for me frantically by now, and I was constantly watching for his form through the corners of my eyes, registering every shadow, every move, waiting for him to pounce on my being again.

My thoughts were frantic, beads of sweat formed on my brow; my heart pounded in my chest. I pondered over what Shan might be doing. I had every reason to believe that he would find me. He must have figured out that I would try to escape. Wouldn't he be on the lookout at the train station? Where else would I go? And how many flights would there be to Ghana anyway? I was sure that his scientific and calculating brain would figure that simple thing out. He would surely be waiting for me at Heathrow. A car could get to the airport faster than a train. He would be furious, and I was not armed to face his wrath. I had a whole night's wait at the airport, and what was more, I was by myself. What if he found me? What if he stopped me? What if he killed me? Thank God I had no luggage to contend with. Please God, I prayed, my eyes wide open, please make this go right for me.

I arrived at Heathrow Airport seven hours before I could board.

The airport was dead at this time of the night, with only a handful of staff on duty. There was not a soul around whom I could call for help, no compassionate face to stand by me. In the semidarkness of a waiting room, I tried not to fall asleep and kept up my vigil. The hours and minutes ticked on, disaster threatening at every moment. At last, the signs of a new day arrived. The call for boarding came. And I cried my way to freedom.

Free Again

My parents were shocked when they saw me. They didn't think they would see me in such dreadful circumstances. How could this have happened to their young, fragrant flower? Why didn't I come home earlier? Why hadn't I called? Most of the time Ma spoke to me in private; Baba listened silently when he was around. Raj was home for the summer and he kept out of my way.

I was glad to be home, but I was ashamed to reveal what had happened to me. To begin with, my parents did not know about the rape. And so I had to tell them about it first.

Ma made no comment and I wondered if she thought it must have been my fault after all. She also did not seem very angry at Shan for the way he had treated me, and I felt ashamed and guilty. Baba of course was quiet.

"Why did you have to tell him anything at all? You should have known better," Ma said to me, annoyed.

"I thought we should start our life with a clean slate, Ma," I replied, feeling defeated.

She saw my bruised arms, but she did not comment on them. How I wanted to cry in her arms, but they were not inviting.

"Why didn't you tell us earlier?" Ma asked.

"Because I couldn't! He would have caught me calling you, and I don't know what he would have done. I was scared."

"Couldn't you just get away and call?"

"No! He didn't allow me to go to the university. I couldn't go anywhere. I hardly had showers, I hardly ate, and all the time I had to keep him calm so he wouldn't get more angry. I was just trying to stay alive and sane."

I was getting more interrogation than sympathy. I don't know what they wanted to hear. Maybe they thought that it was too late—that I was already married to him and nothing could be done now.

Indian society, generally, did not approve of divorce easily. Even if by some odd circumstance a couple separated, it was assumed the woman was at fault. Usually the husband left the wife. Back then and sometimes even now, the role of a loyal wife is ingrained deeply into every girl's mind since childhood, and we were taught that tolerance and sacrifice were virtues above all others.

Shan arrived in Ghana two days later.

He phoned my parents and told them that he was coming to our house. And so Ma told me to go spend a night with the Khetris.

"But I don't even know them!" I protested.

"They are a nice family and she is a lovely lady. I don't know where else you could go."

Perhaps because Mrs Khetri was young, Ma thought I would be relaxed with her and open up. I remember sleeping next to her in her bedroom, which Mr Khatri had been nice enough to vacate for me. I felt strange there. I was withdrawn and found it hard to share my thoughts. I wanted to be left alone. It seemed everyone was older and wiser than me. I felt foolish, inexperienced, and inferior.

However sympathetic Ma and Baba seemed, I agonized about their unspoken judgment of me. Baba left almost all the sorting out to Ma, though perhaps they made joint decisions behind closed doors. I had always tried not to disappoint my parents and could never imagine them thinking of me as a bad daughter. This attitude came from respect, not fear. Living up to their ideals had always been my goal, but it put a heavy toll on me right now. I had been brought up in a protected environment, with a high level of decency. Nobody raised their voices, nobody was ever angry or hurt. Our days at home had flowed evenly, smoothly. Nevertheless, ancient expectations lurked beneath this daily harmonious life. I realize now that I had grown up in surroundings with conflicting demands and contrary cultures—the very Indian upbringing at home and the American culture outside since I was nine. I had to decide for myself what made sense and what did not. To cope, I had compartmentalized my life. I suppose it is up to each young person to figure out what is and is not acceptable. In youth we do not realize the future repercussions of the actions we take.

My parents brought me home the next day from the Khetris' house. I was in no mood to face Shan. I did not like him. He was cruel, insensitive, and malevolent. He had oppressed me for so long that I did not want to be in his presence. But reality caved in upon me.

"Shan's been asking for you," Ma said. "I've told him to come this evening."

Shan came. The worry lines on his forehead looked more prominent; his eyebrows were raised, and his glasses would slide down ever so slightly due to perspiration. He kept wiping the beads of sweat above his lips. I watched, feeling quite numb, not knowing what to expect. Why had he come here? He hated me. What did he want now?

"I'm so, so sorry, Munni. I'll never do that to you again."

"Munni" is what he called me sometimes in affection. It meant "little girl."

"Please, let's be together again, I'm really sorry."

He almost sobbed.

The promises all came from his head, not his heart. Why I felt that way I am not sure. Perhaps because I knew I could not trust him—he did what suited him to serve his current purpose. I could not forget the way he had extracted information from me for his own use—he had lied to find out what I would say and to catch me. He had said what was convenient for him, whether true or not. He had exempted himself from the truth.

In my mind's eye I was witnessing a silent movie. I could see action but not hear words.

Ma had stayed in the room with us.

"Please, I can't live without you. You know that."

He begged, over and over, in a tremulous voice. It didn't matter to him that Ma was present.

I looked at him blankly.

I felt sorry for his distress but could not bring about true compassion. I was in an impossible situation. Ma and Baba would have a lot of explaining to do on my behalf if now they had to find a new husband for me. I didn't want them to have to go through that. They had not paid enough attention to finding my first husband, why would they want to carry this new burden anyway?

Shan came again the next day, and the next. He would make the ends of the earth meet even if it was the last thing he did. He was determined.

"He seems to be genuinely sorry for what he did. And he really wants to make it up to you," Ma said. "Why don't you give him another chance?"

I wanted to believe he was truly sorry, but I couldn't. It was less than a week since I had fled from hell, which had been brought about by this same person who now said he couldn't live without me. I felt as if someone had deliberately pushed me down the stairs and was now asking me if I was okay. Was I supposed to say yes and climb back up with him behind me? My escape from him had unnerved me, and I found it difficult to ignore the last four months. Too many opinions had been formed, and there had been threats whose echoes I could still hear. "I will deal with you," he had told me.

And yet I had no choice.

Ma was always the practical one, on top of all the issues that needed to be dealt with at home. She lectured Shan. She told him sternly that if he ever laid a hand on me again he would have to answer to her. I don't know what else she told him behind closed doors. She obviously believed I had no choice but to go back to him. I think she trusted him and thought his pleas were genuine.

I have often asked myself why my parents did not take a stronger stand and forbid me to go back to him. I could not believe that they did not care or love me enough. For my part, I certainly lacked the experience and knowledge to discriminate between hope and reality. I turned to hope.

Shan's parents never came to know about the rape, or his abuse of me, or even my running away back to Accra. Neither my parents nor I had informed them about the recent events in our lives. Perhaps my parents did not want to bring shame on me; perhaps, because they managed to bring us back together, they had decided to let matters be.

Over the next month in Accra, Shan and I spent happier times. He was attentive and tried to please me. But he needed constant reassurance that I would not leave him. Ma thought it magical that he never left me alone, but for me, trust did not come so easily.

Ma and Baba held a reception for us in Accra and announced to the world that our wedding in India was set for July 16.

A Public Wedding

The marriage ceremony that July in India served as a public announcement of our matrimony; it graced us with blessings from our elders and welcomed us as a married couple in our community. Although not a deliberate secret, our registered marriage had not been public knowledge. I had not bothered to ask my parents if my uncles and aunts in India had known about it—perhaps I would have, if my life had progressed normally. It had been a hurried and unexpected event, and there would have been too much effort required for relatives to accept it at short notice. Only some-one brought up in the confines of an Indian culture can under-stand the nuances that exist within all its systems and rules.

We proceeded to Trivandrum, the capital of Kerala. Kerala is a narrow state, about fifty miles wide and four hundred miles long, along the southwestern Malabar Coast. Because of its location and its wealth in spices, cashews, and tea, it was visited and influenced by many different peoples, especially the Portuguese and the Arabs. Over time the Christian and Muslim populations grew, and one can find many beautiful churches and mosques there in addi-tion to Hindu temples. People speak Malayalam, a language very different from Hindi, my mother tongue. Their food is rice based, unlike the wheat-based diet of the north, and coconut and cane sugar by-products are used extensively in their cooking. It is amaz-ing how advanced the women in Kerala are compared to other places in India; this is perhaps because the state has a history of matriarchy.

The wedding was to take place in Guruvayur, a city in the mid-dle of the state and known for its famous Ayyappan temple. It is a seven-hour drive north from Shan's birthplace, Trivandrum. It is the wish of nearly all Hindu Keralites to be married in this sacred temple. It was Shan's mother's request that we too be married here, and I thought that starting off with God's blessings would be aus-picious.

July was the middle of the rainy season, and the heat lulled the body into lethargy. When we arrived that afternoon, we went straight for worship. The air was sultry and the crowd over-whelming. With blurred streaks of white-clothed people rushing about among the rising vapors of heat, the scene looked as if it were from an impressionist painting. The ground was hot under our bare feet and it felt as if we were doing penance. After doing the three traditional rounds of the huge temple, we proceeded to the altar to pay our respects to the idol.

We then proceeded to take a short walk through a winding

unpaved path to our small motel. We were ushered to the second floor, our luggage in the hands of the driver and some helpers. A bare whitewashed room with a cord-strung bed and *chinchuks* (lizards) on the walls—this was not how I had anticipated spending the night before the formal wedding, despite my recent travails with Shan. This was definitely different from the romantic settings I had always imagined. I wondered what the rest of my life would bring. With slim confidence in my future and no one specific to rely on or turn to, I lost hope in the many things that are taken for granted by most people.

July 16 dawned. The ceremony took place in the morning. Many of Shan's relatives had come to Guruvayur, but since Kerala was far away from Rajasthan, my relatives could not make it. My brother Raj had come and I was glad he was there. Men who enter the temple must be bare chested and wear a shawl-like covering. So Shan, Baba, Raj, and Papa (Shan's father) had to comply, wearing the same white-colored lungi and shawl. Ma dressed me in a red sari, which I had purchased to change into after the wedding, because Amma (Shan's mother) said that the lehenga-choli that is usually worn by brides in Rajasthan could not be worn to the temple. The stand-up ceremony took no more than fifteen minutes, which was unusual compared to the North Indian tradition in which the bride and groom have to remain seated for hours on end while the priest chants the wedding *mantras*. After us, the next bride and groom were ready to be married, and so there continued one wedding after another in the small *mandap* (marriage tent) at the temple.

The following days were spent in Trivandrum, with formal introductions to relatives. This was my first visit to southern India. Obviously I could not speak Malayalam, which is said to be the fastest spoken language in the world. Our wedding was only the second out-of-community marriage in the history of the family, and their curiosity was evident in every raised eyebrow and whispered tone. Since I could not converse with many of the women,

I smiled meekly and accepted their gracious good wishes. Blessings were bestowed upon us when we touched the feet of our elders. Talking to men, although they knew English, was out of the question. Eye contact in such situations is avoided and proximity was only for receiving blessings.

Shan's father had shed his doubts and warmed up to me, and he made the introductions with a proud glow on his face. We drove to his ancestral home. It was further south, in a remote village partly hidden by canopies of inaccessible tropical wilderness. The road was uneven and the bumpy car ride with so many passengers was quite memorable. We came to a vast clearing with a massive wooden house on stilts, built in a slanted architectural style using thick round logs. Every house here seemed to have a well for drinking water and for washing clothes and utensils. Even children were adept at hauling pails of water. A barefoot young boy called Udai showed us around and led us to the edge of the woods. There he pointed to the big orange ball that was the setting sun, saying something I could not understand. From somewhere temple bells could be heard as the evening prayers started. As the three of us walked back toward the house, where dinner was being prepared, I felt myself clinging to the mystical picture made by the tropical sun in the wilderness. I wanted to stay in this quiet moment away from reality. I felt remote and distant, caught between unsettled thoughts of Shan and the onslaught of new events. I needed that orange orb perhaps because it represented a longing for something too far to reach, a miracle in my future life.

When we walked back to the ancestral home, there was a feast ready for us. I couldn't eat the freshly cut chicken, though it was served very respectfully as a special treat. One of Shan's very old aunts sang in English, "Welcome, welcome, O gentleman, welcome welcome O." She had been taught the rhyme in her school days during the British Raj, but she did not seem to understand a word of it.

In the hustle-bustle of family invitations to dinner every day,

Shan and I barely had time to talk. I noticed that he seemed to have a secret history with an older, married cousin of his, who laughed a lot around him and nudged him on a few occasions. Apparently it was okay for him to have his secrets. Our nights together were timid. My personality changed when I was with him—I tended to speak only when asked, held myself back, and did not laugh much. I was not unhappy, but there was an awareness, a consciousness of how circumstances could change without warning. I was aware of how he needed full disclosure, how he planned our lives and how insecure he felt when I was not around.

But I was enjoying the lazy setting of the tropics, living in the thick of nature, listening to the droning of the insects and the chirping of the crickets all night long, watching the rays of the newborn sun as they made their way through the latticed palm leaves into my room. This I needed desperately. It was the only antidote to my reality. There was a strength there that could not be found in the frailty of the human mind, and it offered a profound and deep sense of constancy. Like me, I thought, nature had nothing to gain, it accepted life with ease and grace, but unlike me, nature offered itself at no cost.

On one of our last days there, in Trivandrum, we had to take a taxi back home from the airline office. Shan got in first and settled in the back seat. Then he asked me to get in, saying, "Always let me go in first, because I don't want the driver to run away with you in it."

Was this absurd or was I naïve? I didn't have the answer, but it made me realize how extreme his insecurity was.

I had pleased everyone except myself. I had tried to please my parents, and his. And in pleasing them all, I had accomplished nothing. Of us all, I am the only one left on the planet today. They have all lived and died, but the burden of having forfeited my wants, of having accepted my suffering, still lies on my heart.

We did not have a honeymoon, preferring instead to spend the time with our parents.

"Shan seems to be okay now," Ma told me, looking very pleased. "He loves you so much, he doesn't want to leave you for a moment."

"Yes. I'll be quite fine, Ma. There's really nothing to worry about."

I was lying. He did not stay with me because he loved me, he stayed with me because he just couldn't be without me.

But I did not want to trouble Ma anymore. I felt as if I did not belong to her, as if all my burden was mine alone. I wondered if I really mattered to her in her heart. If I did, then it must not have been enough to change the course of her thoughts. It is a good thing she did not live to see the fatal day that was to come.

Back to England

We returned to England in September for the beginning of the new academic year, and this time we managed to find a studio apartment on the second floor of a duplex, right at the top of a little hill. The windows looked out onto massive trees, a gift to keep the senses alive. I filled the flat with plants and painted the walls green and blue. The carpet, the bedcover, the curtains—every piece had some shade of green in my imaginary jungle.

We led a very steady life, our purpose being university education. Together we fulfilled all the responsibilities of an ordinary, married couple. We were concerned about rent, groceries, bus stops, hot water, my parents, his parents. We talked about heaters, clothes, and stereos. We even discussed where we might immigrate to after Shan finished his studies. Shan had a dry sense of humor, and it lightened up our seriousness now and again. But we never seemed to talk about things that really mattered. We did not talk about our relationship, whether we were happy or discontented with each other. We did not talk about our worries or fears, we didn't buy each other insightful gifts or behave romantically. We never ever talked about the past if we passed the dorm, or ever visited Mrs Sharrock to thank her.

Everything was fine, yet nothing was fine. The two modes of my life coexisted surreptitiously, and it was only a shift in mood that reflected this play of the mind. It is a mystery to me how one inner world tolerated the other. And so, in spite of the peaceful surroundings, I was keenly aware of my unspoken feelings, and the fears that lurked inside me.

I wrote to Ma and Baba regularly. Didi was married and living in Canada, and Raj was busy at university. I wrote to Nandita, my mate in Delhi, and tried to keep in touch with some of my other friends there, but Shan protested.

"What is the point of keeping in touch with all these friends? I don't think you will meet them again."

"If we go to Delhi, I will."

"Yes, but I don't want you to write to your university friends or meet them."

"Why?"

"Why are you asking why? Do you want to write to that old boyfriend of yours too?" His voice rose.

He was jealous of the imaginary devils he had conjured up in his fertile mind. He evidently thought that only by restricting my contacts with other people would he be guaranteed a secure marriage. And of course he did not want anyone to find out about his abusive behavior.

I decided not to challenge him and stopped writing to my friends. My marriage was more important at this point. Perhaps later I would catch up with them. Meanwhile I became lonely and isolated, and I never regained some of them.

Even in the dark of night, when it was time for intimacy, the distance between us would not recede. The rituals of our sex life were performed with little love and certainly no tenderness. They can only be called degrading, for what dignity can actions bring without the accompanying sensitivity and love? They were selfish acts that conveyed humiliation and a deep sense of unwantedness.

In the dark, he wanted to talk about things that I did not want to discuss. Using my past as a spur to his fulfillment, an instrument for his pleasure, he would ask me about *that* degrading event. How could I allow his condescending attitude to flourish in the dark of night, when he could not see my face, when he could feel safe only with the dark thoughts that he had befriended? There were moments of callous indifference and dismissive routines, with traces of cruelty, and they served to deepen the schism between us.

I believe everybody has the ability to behave with sensitivity, but not all of us choose to exercise it openly. Some of us are too shy, or have too much pride, or are too insecure to succumb to such emotion. Shan was a secretive man, in manner and spirit. He would not tell me where he went and when he would be back; it was impossible to read his thoughts through the void of his expressionless face; he never broached any topic remotely connected with his feelings. Perhaps he was afraid that expressing his feelings would shift the balance of power he held in our relationship. So there was no trust.

The physical violence did not start again, but the rift between us was never bridged.

Schoolwork took over my incomplete life. Shan had started his third year of chemical engineering and I pursued a teaching degree. After six months, I started teaching at Barnsley, a small coal-mining town outside Sheffield. I took the bus every day and enjoyed the bumpy but solitary ride.

I taught math and English as part of my teaching probation, and computer concepts were being introduced as part of the curriculum. I decided to take a correspondence course on a hot new topic: Cobol programming. A short course would ensure me a trainee position as a programmer somewhere. It was tough learning for me, but Shan took me to his computer lab at school and we wrote silly Assembler programs and analyzed *Star Trek* quadrants until I understood the concepts. He could be understanding when my need had nothing to do with feelings! I had taken logic as my minor at college, and programming was a newfound joy. My mind was directed at learning, which became a welcome distraction from the dangerous world of emotional turmoil and superficial integrity.

Shan was still in university and it would be three years before he finished his masters degree. I gave up teaching to start my new career in programming, which gave us the extra income we so desperately needed. I earned £120 a week, about half of which went to the rental of our studio apartment, the rest for food and utilities. There was not enough to pay for the old Mini car we wanted, so we took on jobs from time to time, selling door-to-door, collecting pool tickets, even cleaning schools as janitors.

I had come a long way from the world of cocktail parties, sheltered innocence, romantic dreams, and unfettered ambition.

Zambia: An Interlude

Two years after our wedding, I decided I wanted to visit my parents. It was early summer, they had moved to Zambia and my heart ached to be with them. It is customary after marriage for a girl to visit her mother's home for a few months now and then. It would be a blessing for me to be able to unburden my life's inadequacies and trade them for peace, even if only for a few precious weeks.

Shan insisted that he should come too. He *would not* stay apart from me. This was to become a pattern in my life with him. I never understood his obsession to be with me all the time. He said that if he did not come he would be worried about me. Worried about what? In the beginning it was easy to accept his claim. He *was* a worrier, and there was very little reason for me to doubt him: I was just not clever enough to figure out that he worried about issues that were not even on my radar screen.

We had a grand family reunion. It had been a long time since

Raj, Didi, and I were together. I wish that we had infused those carefree days of reminiscing with deeper conversations of the heart that would have helped us to help each other, at that time and in the future. But it was easier to shy away and skirt the surfaces of our existence, and like most people that was where we hovered, never venturing to discuss our deep dark secrets with one another. Summer came to an end, and we headed back to Sheffield.

Canada: A New Home, A New Life

I had worked in England for three years and Shan was in the last year of his masters program. England was a place where we could survive, but not thrive. We began to look at opportunities in Canada and the United States and decided on the former. Immigration would not be difficult for us: we were both skilled in areas that were in great demand. But I would miss the natural beauty of South Yorkshire, with its vast moors, where Shan and I had spent many hours during the weekends. Shan would fly his kites, and I would become lost in the world of the ragged cliffs, from where I could watch the hand gliders in the distance, pushing themselves off.

We rejoiced when our immigration application for Canada was approved. Anxious to start our new adventure, we decided to leave as soon as Shan finished his last exam. But first we had to find some way to get there on our meager savings. We sold a few things, gave others away, and managed to ship a small crate of goods to await us in Canada. We auctioned off our car at a local fair and raised enough money to ensure two one-way airline tickets.

On the day following Shan's last university exam, we dashed off to the airport, ready to take a cheap standby flight to Toronto. We had to wait overnight outside the airline offices before we found a flight to take us to our new home.

A new home, a new way of life. For the first time I felt more than a little hopeful about my future.

Four

Life's Unfolding

ORDEAL BY FIRE

Settling Down

Iexperienced the wonder of a Canadian autumn—a brilliant
display of rich colors set off beautifully against a bright clear
sky. It had been a long summer and the first snow arrived only
at the very end of the year, an exception by which I disappointed-
ly measured the onset of every subsequent winter. We had decided to make Toronto our home, and it did not take long for Shan
and me to find good jobs in software development. We lived in a
fourteen-story suburban apartment with a good view, and we
acquired a brand new Impala. The change in life and lifestyle was
welcome. Suddenly there was luxury in our lives. I remembered
from my younger days what they said about moving west.

The newness of the country was a welcome distraction from
the strains of our married life. After four years ours was still a
mechanical existence, and I was no closer to knowing Shan or
understanding his true nature. I had been looking for something
deeper, something more profound in him, but I never succeeded.

Although he was not unfriendly, Shan was awkward and
uncomfortable in social settings. With his reserved nature and
preference for an exclusive lifestyle, I was being isolated without
realizing it. What I imagined to be small compromises now began
to lead to huge tests of mental endurance. In my belief of good
over evil, I let all things ride, taking no action, hoping that good
would fall on me like a ripe fruit from an aged tree.

His insecurities could have been addressed through love, but he
did not seek love. The dark silence of the nights did nothing to
help my cause; on the contrary, the lack of a loving sexual relationship became the most unbearable aspect of my life. Neither of
us risked openness, and we carried on with sexual practices that we
could not alter. I accomodated him because I could not ignore
him. He wanted me to make up fanciful and coarse stories to stim-
ulate him; he wanted me to whisper them in his ear so he could

81

please himself. This obligatory and unreciprocated act left me feeling used. Anger at his insensitivity and my unfulfillment would settle in my throat; sometimes I sobbed. And he would be fast asleep, accustomed to these lifeless routines.

The First Child: Nina

We both wanted children, and now that we were settled, we could move on with this new phase of our lives. I had dreamt of having a baby to shower my love upon, an emotion which had been dormant for far too long.

Our first child, Nina, was born two years after we came to Canada. This was singularly the most overwhelming event of my life. The wonder of wonders. A tenderness overtook my entire being, and the body's reaction to the tenderness was visible in breasts overflowing with milk, and in the protective cavity of the arms. I would shudder from a sense of profound love and at the marvel of the unfathomable mystery of creation. Shan's ecstasy paralleled mine, he was a proud father.

I had wanted to call her Nandita, after my friend whom I could not write to, but we settled for Nina.

Eventually I started work again, juggling my different responsibilities. Life became more complex. Shan was inept at domestic duties and even in Sheffield he had left the housework to me. Now, despite my pleas for help, he chose to disregard the many chores that needed to be done in our life. Arguments were only a waste of time. He could wear down a mountain with his sheer persistence.

One evening, as on many other occasions, I came home overwrought and fatigued from work at the office and the long subway and bus rides. We only had one car. I needed help with groceries, with Nina, and with housework. Shan was not home, but he phoned afterwards. "Listen, I have to work late, and I don't know what time I'll be back," he said. He came at one.

"I was trying to reach you at the office," I told him the next morning.

"It's hard to get hold of me because I'm in the lab, and the phones don't roll over," he replied.

"Well, what if it's an emergency and I need to get hold of you?"

"Call security, and they may be able to find me, but try not to do that —it's too complicated."

Okay, I thought, so much for that.

Sometimes he would be playing squash, or hanging around with the boys at work.

"Where did you go?" I would ask when I felt daring. He was never specific about the places he went to.

"Why do you want to know? Can't I have a drink with a friend without you complaining about it?"

"You can at least let me know where you are and when you'll be back."

"I don't know *when* or *where* I'll go," he said, irritated. "We make plans at the last minute." His voice would get louder with every response until I would feel that any further provocation would blow his fuse. I had to be aware of his limits and cater to them.

He insisted that I take Nina with me wherever I went—I should never be alone. I knew that it was not for Nina's sake but for mine that he insisted that I phone him whenever I reached my destination. And he demanded I be back at specified times. Delays had to be explained, and the response then was anger.

"Where have you been? Why didn't you come back on time? What were you doing?"

"I got delayed shopping—that's all."

"Are you sure that's all you were doing?"

"Yes! What did you expect I was doing?"

"I don't know—you could be doing anything." When he talked like that, it seemed he was implying I had boyfriends. But I had no friends at all except Marlee, from work, who would come over sometimes.

I found myself forming a field of self-awareness that could not be shared with him. I could not deny this other self, which channeled my spirit towards a much needed expression. To survive the harshness of my unforgiving world and revive that inner peace, I needed the inner sanctum of my soul. How strange it is that we find in ourselves another hidden world, away from even the closest of our partners.

I escaped into myself every chance, every moment I had. I found a haven in this world of solitude, filled with the pleasures of art and poetry. I wrote much, but what I wrote was far too precious to be revealed. Read outside its context, I feared, it would have no meaning. "The real with its meaning read wrong and emphasis misplaced, becomes the unreal," says Tagore. If my husband could not know me at face value, how could he possibly understand me an inch deeper?

One morning I received news that Baba had had a heart attack. Raj, my brother, phoned me from Detroit, where he had settled the previous year. To protect me from too great a shock, both Raj and Shan told me that Baba was sick, but later that day Shan sat close to me and broke the news of Baba's death. I was devastated, but the tears would not come. While Shan did not grieve, he was there to console me, and I was reminded that he could be sensitive and sympathetic if he wanted. He could be kind and loving and gentle toward me during times of distress. I wished that I could bring that out from him more often.

Baba had retired in Jodhpur, India, where he became the Vice Chancellor of Jodhpur University. It had taken my parents two long years to build a beautiful home. Baba's ambitions for building a model village in rural India died with him. I wanted desperately to go back to India but we could not afford three tickets, and my going alone was out of the question. I could not leave Nina with Shan—he would not know what to do. Besides, with his insecurities and his suspicions, he would not have liked me to go alone.

My mother was always a strong woman. She had been active in helping to raise the status of women in Jodhpur through various organizations, but Baba's death wore out her spirit and soon afterwards she fell ill and suffered two heart attacks. Raj and his wife, Sweety, went to India to look after Ma.

Widowhood in India is not easy; the woman is subjected to immense grief from others, even if she can hold her own. The time allocated for mourning overwhelms one into a depressing mood, even if one is able to bear the heartache of losing a beloved life partner.

A few years after Baba's death, having suffered from several complications, Ma died in her sleep. I was keenly aware that both my parents were gone from my life forever. Although I felt that their love for me had been limited by many factors, they had taken away with them the umbrella of familyhood, and with it any remnant of support. My sister, also in Toronto, and my brother, who returned back to Detroit, were my only family now. I was not sure how much Ma had told them about my troubled existence with Shan. I myself had not shared this with them. My sister was busy with her own extended family, and my brother, I felt, was not ready to face the burden of my marital problems. So while they lived close by, they had only the remotest idea of my dire situation.

I inherited from my parents a sum of money, which I hoped to put to good use.

"I was thinking of buying a new car—an Audi," Shan told me, soon after the money arrived.

"You don't need a new car!" I retorted, furious that he would consider using the money toward the purchase of something so extravagant.

"If we get a new car, then *you* can use the Impala," he said, trying to buy me with the old car.

"I don't need it. I'd rather put the money toward our mortgage or something useful."

We were no longer in the apartment, having bought a new home after Nina's birth.

We had a joint bank account. As in most Indian families, marriage meant sharing everything, and there was no question of having separate finances, because that indicated a lack of trust.

And so one day he told me to come with him to a dealer to check out the car he had bought. I could only challenge him so far, and my limit had been reached. It was natural self-preservation that kept me from prodding and poking, provoking him further.

And the fracture of our marriage grew underneath the surface as we led our superficial lives.

He got the Audi and I was given the Impala.

Spy in the House

Shan loved the good life. It was something he wanted for himself, not simply for prestige or for keeping up. We were earning well, and there was nothing lacking in our material world. We moved into our second home. It seemed to me that amidst all the luxury, the joy of a relationship, of trust, of warmth and of kindness was nonexistent. It was a sad realization that material progress was not a measure of inner contentment. I yearned for a loving partner.

One evening as I went about in the family room, vacuuming the floor and untangling the cords of the telephone, I came across something that broke every strand of trust that I may ever have preserved for him. Hidden away underneath the brown couch was a tape recorder. A wire ran from the recorder to the phone on the side table next to the couch. My first reaction was confusion, and then I understood. He was recording phone conversations. I was furious and humiliated. When he came back from work, I waited upstairs in the bedroom. Nina was asleep.

"How can you do this? Why are you recording my telephone conversations?"

"It's nothing, I just want to know who calls while I am away.

Why, do you have anything to hide?"

It was grand, the way he turned the tables around!

"I can't live with you if you behave like that!" I said angrily.

Without a second thought, he retorted scornfully: "Well, you'll just have to stay and suffer, won't you?"

I asked him what else he was doing. I accused him of everything I could. I thought to myself, I'm not going to stay with him anymore, and I don't really care if I say all the things I have ever wanted to say.

"You have a rotten mind! You think you're a lion but you're really a mouse! You know that? You master manipulator! You control freak!"

"Shut up, bitch! I'm warning you—don't start a fight!" he shouted.

"Is there anything else you know how to do?… How can you? You're too busy with your friends, visiting strip clubs on Airport Road!"

"Munni, I told you already, stop it! You're a cheap slut. I knew I should never have married you!"

"No, I won't stop! I don't care what I say—I'm not staying with you anyway!"

We went on and on. I said anything and everything that came to my mind, and so did he. This was an ugly fight—it wasn't just name-calling—it was deep down, it was how we felt, that was coming out—hurtful, repressed feelings of betrayal and anger. We must have fought a good two hours. Exasperated, I said to him that I wanted out of the marriage. It was then that he calmed down.

"I'm sorry, babe, really I am." He called me "babe" from time to time, specially when he wanted to make up.

"I still want to leave, I can't take stuff like this anymore."

"Please Munni, I am sorry."

I kept quiet. I wanted nothing to do with him. But he thought I was only bargaining.

He was coarse and cruel, and I knew that the motives behind him wanting me to stay were purely selfish. He needed me to keep house and earn money. But most of all he needed me for his social prestige, because losing face was the worst thing that could happen to him. If I walked out on him, he would have to answer to society, to his parents. It would be devastating. Outwardly we were a perfect couple. I had overheard a family friend teasing him about how he had me under perfect control; this, apparently for that friend, meant a perfect marriage. Shan had beamed at the comment.

"I'll change, I'll do whatever you want," he pleaded.

"No, you won't. You're saying that now, and tomorrow you'll be back to your old self."

"Please, babe, just one more chance."

It was two a.m. now and we had been going at it for more than three hours. My timing had been right. The last thing I had wanted was an argument that kept me from feeding Nina or tending to her, and I was glad I did not have to deal with that. I had chosen to challenge him at night, in the bedroom.

But I was exhausted.

I wanted to get away and clear my head. I needed oxygen. As I walked toward the door, Shan came and blocked it. He knew that I could phone a lawyer, the police, or anyone once I was out of his sight. He was careful not to leave me in a state where I could harm him in any way.

"Please, just one more chance. I love you," he begged, holding my arms, blocking the door with his body.

I could not force myself out of the room; and I could do nothing else, even prepare to sleep, until I gave in. It was a simple strategy he had, and unlimited stamina. He also had the advantage of a good memory, so he could remember my failings from the past, which he could put to use in his arguments. And so, in our dark room, with a lighted bedside lamp in the far corner, he regained my "trust," and once again hope for the future reared its deceptive ways. Over the next hour or two, he managed gradually to turn me around—kneeling on the carpet directly in front of me as I sat on the side of the bed, putting his hands on my thighs or my arms, looking into my face, waiting for me to say something, talking to me softly, rather than kissing me or putting his arms around me, saying, "Please, Munni, please." He never gave in completely—only just enough.

When I did come around, he made me promise that I would never again bring up the subject of leaving him.

"I don't want you ever to talk about leaving me again," he said, in a low husky tone. "I'll go berserk if you do that, babe, you know I don't like to hear that."

The next few days he was a bit better, but then my life continued as before, controlled by his whims. At this time my work required me to travel, and I had long arguments with him to get his permission. His jealousy was boundless. I cannot say that I was resigned to my fate but I had long told myself I had to have patience. My frustrations after all were only due to one individual, and I took solace in Richard Lovelace's lines learnt long ago at school:

Stone walls do not a prison make,
Nor iron bars a cage;
Minds innocent and quiet take
That for a hermitage;
If I have freedom in my love,
And in my soul am free,
Angels alone that soar above
Enjoy such liberty.

And so I was never defeated. But what was I being patient for?

Shan was happiest when he participated in activities. He enjoyed outings such as picnics and camping. He would smile and be full of humor during those hours of carefree fun. He loved boats and was drawn to water. He did not like to be by himself, always wanted his family physically around him; and yet he was always within his own little world. As far back as I can remember he always sat in his favorite corner of the couch. Game shows were a favorite of his. He would want his meals there, never fussed about what he ate, only about where he ate, and he would be there until bedtime, which was usually one a.m. And *then*, he would expect me to wait up for him. For what? Blind performance that loses its sweetness in the emptiness of solitary pleasure.

Even now it is difficult for me to understand the workings of his mind. One assumes that there were reasons, there was a logic to why he behaved the way he did; but Shan was too secretive for me even to begin unraveling his mystery. His actions oscillated between a settled indifference toward me and a more aggressive resentment that was impossible for him to shake off. This under-current lingered under the surface of our absorbed and busy lifestyle. The past was captive inside him and there were burdens that were too complex and intricate to resolve. I know that the rape was something he never forgave me. I assumed he found the outlets for his frustrations and needs in other ways. I didn't know what they were, but he stayed away from home too much for me to think of it as normal.

His childhood, I thought, did reflect his behavior somewhat. His father was studying away from home when Shan was born. Shan first saw his father only when he was three years old. Amma told me that Shan was so protective of her at that time that he would not let his father go near her. Shan also had a younger brother, Kris, of whom he was always intensely jealous. Kris, ten years younger, was more outgoing and had a softer nature. In their home, Papa, though not dominant in a loud way, was unques-tionably the authoritative figure in the family, and Amma, while not a weak person, took pride in her subservient role. Shan often complained that Papa did not pay attention to him. But these biographical facts are not so unusual; some are commonplace.

They certainly do not easily explain his compulsiveness, which tormented me for so long.

Vijay and Andy

Our son was born on May 28, 1986. This was a time when I glimpsed a fleeting happiness that contributed greatly to the approaching turning point in my way of thinking.

I had risen fast in the corporation I worked for, and this I attributed to the hard work and diligence that I had learnt from my father. Heavy workloads occupied my hours, and there was very little time for friendships. There was however, relief in a particular relationship, a peculiar meeting of the minds. Andy McKenzie, an external consultant, worked with me on a project at the office. At times we worked together closely for hours, and there was much satisfaction in these interactions. In the many months together, I had discovered his sense of humor, his considerate gestures, and there grew gradually between us a mutual appreciation and fondness. I discovered in myself a confidence due to his kind attitude and admiration for my work. We were intellectual friends and shared easy conversations about our wants, our goals, and our thoughts. We joked about visiting New York together, or perhaps going to a local theatre. Although the relationship was close, it did not induce me to burden him with my difficulties. I was badly in need of affection, but I could not risk Andy's fondness turning into pity. I did not want a relationship based on compassion—that would hardly be the right kind of loving, I thought, still clinging to my idealistic beliefs.

The friendship deepened, and I did not feel the need to reconcile it with my married status. The physical attraction was there, but opportunities were avoided: I was too fearful to start something that could end in tragedy—for him or me. Knowing Shan, the consequences could be unbearable. Andy could hardly have guessed how raw and lifeless my situation was at home. I had fallen in love and was pulled two ways. I could have left Shan, but Andy was not expecting that. I seemed to have lost track of how much of what I thought about was real, and how much of it was yearning and imagination.

I became a happier person, though, and looked forward to each new day. My moods were obviously visible to Shan, and he took notice of my newfound optimism. He started to question me constantly. If I left early, he became curious. If my long hair was down, he was bothered. He called me more frequently at work. He was hardly a jealous man when it came to worldly possessions, but for possession of *me,* he could tear down a mountain. But in spite of our unhappy marriage, the need for another child was never questioned. And so my husband and I were expecting our second child. Nina was five.

My unfulfilled relationship with Andy came to an abrupt end when he announced he had to leave. He left Canada to fulfill his ambitious dreams. I had expected him to move, but not so soon. I was half devastated and half thankful. One of the few people I cared for had left me. Not simply left me, but left me incomplete. But when he left, he presented me the most beautiful card, with the most precious words—a message that conveyed thanks for a very special friendship, and how much he would miss me, and joked about the trips we planned that never materialized.

It did not take long for Shan to find Andy's card—he must have rummaged through my briefcase and papers.

I denied his accusations, which were not actually true, but how could I deny that I had been attracted?

Vijay's birth was difficult: he was a breach baby, like Nina. I had chosen to have a local anesthetic and stay conscious, and Shan had remained with me in the operating room. He peered at me from time to time as I lay under the bright florescent lights, attended by the doctors and nurses. There were complications due to internal hemorrhaging. But I felt intensely happy and contented. I had a little boy!

Suddenly, in one split second, when the doctors and nurses had withdrawn for a few moments, Shan bent down and quietly whispered:

"Is this baby mine?"

My heart dropped a thousand feet.

I looked up at him, and he repeated the question, this time sounding a little bolder.

I didn't say anything.

"We have to keep her in here for a while to ensure she is out of danger, and then you can talk to her," Dr Paradeau said sternly to Shan. Perhaps he had overheard Shan, or perhaps that was only his doctor's manners during an emergency.

I tried to ignore the situation and act as if I did not care about a thing. The world was falling apart on its own, without my trying. If the tears were streaming down to my ears, it was because of Shan's behavior, not the joy of Vijay's birth.

I thought I would have the next few days alone in the hospital—I was wrong. Shan decided to stay with me in the room twenty-four hours a day, sleeping bag and all. I did not want him near, but there he was. He asked me why the baby's eyes were gray. I told him they weren't, the baby's eyes were still glazed from the birth. He was wearing me down. He didn't care that the hospital staff did not leave enough food for the two of us—he had most of it. Shan had no responsibilities at home, his mother was with Nina. She and her husband were living with us at the time.

We left the hospital four days after the delivery. Shan drove and I held Vijay close on my lap. As we approached our home, Shan turned into the parking lot of the mall nearby and parked discreetly at the far end of an empty space.

He wanted to have a talk.

"Can't we talk at home?" I sighed. "What do you want to talk about, anyway?" With the poor tiny baby on my lap and the heat of the midday sun shining through the windshield, I did not have the strength to argue. I sat there for more than four hours listening to Shan's suspicions. My only comfort was the sensual closeness of the baby. I felt certain Vijay could sense every nerve in my body, every tremor in my voice.

"It took long for the administrative work to be done. There was a long lineup," Shan explained to his parents when we returned.

"But you phoned to say you were leaving by ten, it's now three o'clock," his father scolded.

It was then I decided, once again, that enough was enough; I had to get away.

When we came to our room, I lay the baby on the bed.

"I can't live with you," I said quietly. "It doesn't matter if I have a small baby, I'll manage fine."

He lost his mind. "I told you not to say that!" he said, advancing in a threatening way towards me.

I walked past him to the walk-in closet, away from the baby.

"I told you, I never want to hear that!" he shouted.

I turned to face him but kept quiet. I took a step back.

A fist came flying at me, hit my upper arm. I stumbled back between the hangers and clutched at the clothes for support.

And another blow came, hitting my other arm.

"Now I am definitely leaving," I muttered under my breath, but loud enough for him to hear. This was the first time he had hit me in a long time.

"No—I'm sorry—I didn't mean it, okay? I didn't mean it, I'm sorry," he said, a little startled. "Are you okay? Maybe you need to rest. I'll ask Amma to cook something for you."

It was obvious to my in-laws that we were more than just quarreling. They were trying not to interfere, but as I walked into the hallway downstairs, my father-in-law saw the bruises on my forearm and confronted me.

"Did my son hit you?" he asked me, swiftly touching my arm.

"Yes—he's upset." I did not want to talk to Shan's father about our days in Sheffield, but everything was connected to that and it was hard for me to give reasons for Shan's behavior. Papa, especially, and Amma were always considerate of me and I loved them dearly.

"He's angry with me right now," I said.

"About what?"

"He's angry because I want to leave him. He won't let me go."

Papa said nothing to me, but when Shan came down, he said: "Let her go if she wants to."

But Papa got the silent treatment, the blank stare, so familiar to me.

Several months later, Shan again hit me. Nina walked into the room to see him holding me down on the floor. "Call the police," I called out to her; he told her not to, in his loud voice, and she stood there frozen with fear. Finally I sent her away.

Once more I buckled. I couldn't leave him because I feared his rage; I knew that he was quite capable of following me, stalking me and making the independent life I dreamed of unbearable. Any hope I had of him mending his ways was long gone. But I vowed to myself this time that I would give my marriage a ten-year lease: I would be ready to leave when my son was ten. That was an absurd decision, but I wonder if my fate would have been any different had I walked away from the marriage then.

The Joy of Children and More Thoughts of Liberation

Beneath Shan's quietness lay a deeply suppressed restlessness. He was convinced, without a doubt, that nothing could alter the little world around him that carried out his every whim unquestioningly. That was the faith he possessed in my fear. His smiles and laughter, although frequent, hid a different madness dormant inside him. His mind seemed to drift directionlessly, mocking me.

Vijay's young face was a carbon copy of Shan's, except for his little dimples. He was growing up to be a quiet, thoughtful, and happy boy. He loved what all boys loved—sports, music, food. His generosity was overwhelming. Whenever children younger than him visited us, he would give away his stuffed toys and Nintendo games. When he realized a baby could not walk, he would get down on his knees and crawl. He was sensitive to the arts. Once when Nina was performing at a dance concert, Vijay had pointed to the sarangi, an ancient Indian instrument, and whispered in my ear, "Can I play that, Mom?" He had no idea what it was, just that he loved the haunting sound of the stringed instrument. I knew that day that he had a huge part of me in his soul. He could relate to the subtlety of life with a gentleness that showed through his almond-shaped eyes—eyes that turned just a little downward at the edges. I took every chance I got to point out to him the greatness of the sky and the beauty in a flower. I knew that boys needed to be reminded of this more than girls and so I drilled into him all that would make him balance his boisterousness with his gentle side. Later he would tell *me*, to look at the moon or feel the breeze.

Nina too was growing up a beautiful and sensitive child. She had learnt delightful manners, exuding a calm confidence and a surety that would stay with her through the years. Amma once said with pride that when Nina was born, some Indian astrologers had predicted that she would be a great scholar and source of strength for her mother.

Shan's love was evident for both the children—he bought them gifts, and he made them laugh. He would tease them. I remember once when we had all wanted to eat out at different restaurants, he had apparently written down their names on separate pieces of paper, folded them, and asked Vi to pick out one to decide where we should go. Dad won. Of course he then revealed that all the papers had the same name on them!

Shan developed Vijay's inherent love for sports, and before long Vijay was active in practically every aspect of athletics. They spent many hours playing together. Shan was a good engineer and imparted his love of mechanics and gadgetry to his son.

Sometimes during weekends we all went for outings, away from the city if we could. During those trips, Shan never drove—he preferred to sit in the back with a walkman or a VCR hooked to a ten-inch TV he brought with him. Still, the outings were fun; Shan would be out of his dark moods, oblivious to his inner despair.

Such were the happy times in our marriage; I cannot deny they existed, especially after Vijay was born, but they were few and far between. Other times the torments went on—the constant scolding, and arguments, the suspicions, the threats, the physical violence, the absences from home. When he decided he would invest in properties, I had no choice but to yield. In the end his recklessness drained us of all our savings.

Nina and Vijay were slowly becoming sensitive to Shan's behavior and tone towards me. Once, at the age of three, Vijay scolded his Dad from the back seat of the car, saying very boldly, "Don't talk to my Mom like that!" Dad had not replied.

One evening, the kids and I were to meet up with Shan after work so that we could go out together for dinner. We waited for him in the minivan in a prearranged parking lot. Fifteen minutes, half an hour passed. He arrived finally, an hour late. I asked what took so long, the kids had been getting restless to eat.

"You know how much traffic there is at this time," he said irritated.

"You know how much traffic there is too, didn't you make an allowance for it?"

"Don't fight with me. See what you've done? You spoilt my mood now."

"Nina and Vi have homework and they are really hungry—let's go."

Getting behind the wheel, he said, "Why did you do that? You really put me in a bad mood."

"For asking why you are late?"

Shan wouldn't start the car. Nina and Vijay were in the back, waiting, not saying a word.

Fed up, I said to Shan: "Okay, I'm sorry. Let's stop fighting now."

"No, you don't mean it. I want you to mean it."

"I'm really really sorry," I said.

The children said, "Let's go Dad—we're hungry."

We left and went to Gerrard Street, India Town.

The kids got out but Shan started a discussion with me.

He would not leave the argument—and he controlled the locks of the car.

Two and a half hours passed as the children hung outside, playing near a tree and on the sidewalk, saying to each other how much they hated Dad. They were just four and nine.

He always came first, before even the children. Both the children would side with me, but they were too young to fight his ways. If he shouted to Vijay to come downstairs to change the tape in the VCR, Vijay would comply. If Shan wanted juice, or salt in his food while he ate in the family room, they would leave their homework to serve him. If he called them stupid and idiots, because they asked for help with their math homework, they would bear it. If they had to miss going somewhere special because he wanted to sleep in, they would simply have to wait for another opportunity.

It became more and more difficult to negotiate anything with him. If I wanted to disagree with any of his plans, I would need to make a serious case. He never got involved with the kids' karate, or dance, or music lessons. Arguments with him would lead to more useless arguments, until both of us had lost the original point. I had no appetite left for compromise, I was worn out.

To save myself, I turned to books, lectures, and deep introspection. I asked older people—friends' mothers and spiritual advisers—what one should do in such a situation, without telling them the story of my life. The more I read and heard and understood, the stronger I became. I would never expect my own children or my friends to accept this violence to themselves, so why was I yielding to it? If the legendary Jhansi ki Rani could fight a whole army, could I not fight a single man? I had become an embarrassing role model to my own children. Even Nina had asked me why I put up with Dad's behavior. She was not given to flippancy, and I respected her judgment. Her words would hold much weight in my near future.

Thoughts of liberation went spinning in my mind. The more intolerant Shan became, the easier it was for me to justify freedom. To myself, I seemed more determined. I was even overcoming my fear and dread of what he might do in his madness, if I left. I asked myself over and over again, "Could I continue living like this for the next twenty-two years of my married life?"

Five

Life on the Edge

Decision Time

It was October 1996. My professional work was challenging and enjoyable. I was managing a development department in a large corporation, and because the field was expanding and lucrative, I was bursting with new ideas. I put tremendous pressure on myself and I worked ceaselessly to advance professionally. Work was a welcome change from the trying life at home. Unfortunately, though, along with the excitement in the workplace came what seemed to me were destructive office politics, with which I had to cope as well.

The children were back in school after a busy summer. Every evening at home was crammed with routines. I seem to remember from early childhood what the word "routine" meant. We *really* had a routine then, consisting of ordered activity; but in these modern times in Toronto, routine was more like organized chaos: decisions to be made every day, forms to be filled to deadlines, trips to the shops for this project or that, an endless stream of hurried activity. Like a dam, the housework kept building up, and Shan had no inclination to help me.

He usually came home after ten o' clock. More often than not, I would not know where he had been because I was fast asleep when he came, and he woke after the kids and I left. The happy family interludes were fewer now, and there was little interaction between him and the three of us. He interacted with the children when he thought they needed disciplining. He liked to exercise his authority over them. The children hardly spoke to him, unwilling to deal with his angry outbursts, insults, and irritability.

And so he missed out on the children's growing up, sharing with them their thoughts, their struggles, their joys and pains. They were both good children and stayed out of trouble, and I did not have to deal with any school or social crises. I would be exhausted daily but for the children I spared no effort. I had stopped asking Shan about his whereabouts; doing so would have upset the delicate balance of our daily lives.

I presumed there were things he did that he did not want me to know about. I suspected he was out with his friends from his workplace, at a bar or a club, but I had no real idea what was happening in his life away from home. There were no clues that I could see when he came home, and there were no phone calls for him. But I was beyond caring. Even if he had been with another woman, which could have been entirely possible, I was only too glad that he was out of the house. Our time together in bed had become worse than sparse. We had not had sex for years.

One day I came across a cash advance transaction from a casino in the previous month's bank statement. I questioned him. Annoyed, he dismissed it as a "fun" night with the boys at work. But I knew that there was more to it than that—I found a record of a similar transaction in the next statement. Our finances were desperate. The three houses that Shan had invested in years ago had fallen in price, and Shan and his real-estate partners were being harassed for collection by the small mortgage companies that had lent them money. He was in serious debt, which was rapidly becoming unmanageable. Shan had never involved me in this wild scheme, but now I saw hundreds and thousands of dollars being withdrawn from our bank account every month. And, to make more money to pay the huge debts, he had taken to gambling at casinos.

Shan returned home later and later at night. Nina, Vijay, and I would remain tense, knowing that when he came the atmosphere would somehow become unpleasant. The children hated him for his uncaring, bossy attitude. The whole week before I had made up my mind finally to "act," he was out till the wee hours of the morning.

On November 8, I happened to run into a lawyer, Samantha, the older sister of my friend Anita who used to work with me. I bombarded her with questions. At first the questions were coy, but it did not take long for me to absorb the answers and start sketching out some thoughts. Previously, on many occasions, I had thought simply of "leaving" Shan; but I had never seriously considered *divorce*, and I was astounded at the options that were open to me. I asked whether mutual consent was required for a divorce, and how much time and effort the procedure would take. I had not even realized that the legal option of separation was available to me, or that mutual consent was not required. I thought Shan might perhaps agree to a separation. It would give him time to get used to us not being together, and it would free me from his callous ways.

I have no doubt in my mind that all things happen for a reason. I had learnt ancient Vedantic philosophies from the spiritual Vedic texts and from gurus, and the law of karma is a well-known part of the teaching. It states that everything that happens in the present is a result of our past actions, and everything that will happen in the future is a result of our present actions. I knew there was a consequence to every little thought and action that I performed. It became obvious to me that the same logic (every action has a reaction) that held in the material world of physics also held in the subjective world of emotions and thoughts.

Therefore I figured that fate must have thrust me into Samantha's presence. Like a revelation, it was clear to me now what I needed to do. The fear of Shan had suddenly vanished, and I did not care about anything else but to be released from the suffocation that had become my life, from the fear and manipulation and abuse, the disregard and inconsideration not only of me but also of the children.

I had to break away from Shan. How much I had already suffered became clear to me. I did not want the children to be brought up in that home anymore. I did not want them to think this was how normal people lived. I had to surface for air, I could no longer contain myself in the sordid muddy swamp in which I had existed. Now was more than the right time to break away into the light.

How wrong I had been to think that by tolerating all I would be granted a better plane of existence. My biggest weakness was my perception of the problem as merely a huge nuisance. We easily convince ourselves that the problems at home are the challenges of everyday life. And so, what if there is no intimate relationship with one's spouse? What if he gets furious from time to time? What if I have to do all the work? Don't all couples have problems? My upbringing reinforced qualities of tolerance and compassion. Besides, I detested conflict and would do anything to avoid it. And so I had resigned myself to the fact that things could have been worse, and I was still capable of pulling through unpleasant situations. It was a curse to have had an inordinate amount of tolerance.

Now I had to act on my newfound conviction—that I should be true to myself, but not unjust to others. This was the final decision. No one could have dissuaded me from it.

I decided I would tell Shan about my decision on December 1; meanwhile, I would prepare myself. I needed to get the papers ready before I broke the news to him. If I didn't do that, he had the will and the stamina to hold me back. How he would respond was fairly predictable.

There also needed to be a delicate balance in all aspects pertaining to Nina and Vi: between what they needed to know and what would fill them with apprehension, between taking my side and being impartial, between being passive and playing an active role during the divorce. A week after my decision, I took the children, now ten and fifteen, to McDonald's. Samantha, the lawyer, was present and set the stage for what I was to say to them. Her presence alone would establish a seriousness. They would be explained that what was about to happen was not just between me and Dad, but involved the whole family. She would reduce their fears if they felt threatened. She seemed easy to talk to and was ready to listen to their doubts. When I told them about my decision, they were surprised—they never thought that I would actually take a stand and *do something*. Nina felt relief for me. She was fifteen and could sympathize with my years of struggle. She had seen and understood much of what I had gone through. Vijay, because he was younger, was more worried about what would happen. What should he do if Dad came after school to take him? What if Dad started shouting? He asked all his questions with a concerned expression, crying on and off. They listened, and responded with sympathy. It was a natural instinct for them to have compassion for their mother, whom they had seen distressed far too often. I told the children that I would break the news to their Dad in less than two weeks, and until then, they must respect my wish not to disclose my plans. They agreed and waited.

I know Vijay was particularly saddened by the news of the divorce. I later found out that he had said to his teachers, "Please excuse me if you see me sad, it's because my parents are getting divorced."

A Victorious Start

It was Sunday morning, the day I was to break the news to Shan. I was anxious, dreading having to deal with the issue of divorce, and at the same time looking forward to being free of Shan. It was a cold day but the sun's warmth gave me inspiration and courage. I had slept well and was ready to face the unpredictable test. Nina and Vijay were also anxiously waiting, wondering what the outcome would be. They were not scared, just nervous. I asked them to stay in the adjoining room until I finished speaking to their Dad in the family room. They could listen in if they wanted. Having Nina and Vijay in the next room would ensure safety for all three of us—violence could not be dismissed. In fact, it was the expected response. The only thing that would prevent violence was that we were outside the confines of the bedroom, so Shan could not hold me back by force or block the doors.

The previous night we had gone to his office Christmas party and he had commented on how quiet I had been throughout the evening. He had asked what the matter was, why I was unusually quiet. I made up an excuse. It was one of the few times he noticed my silent withdrawal. I had been thinking of nothing else but the next morning. After all these years, I thought, I would have it no other way. I remembered the numerous occasions when he had *promised* me, coerced me into believing in him. How many times had I told him that I wanted to leave. And how many times had he sweet-talked me out of it. There had been moments of fretting, crying, shouting, despair, helplessness. Every time, his pleading ʾ had been merely a way of ending a fight, not resolving the issues through understanding and discussion.

There were many things I did to arm myself ahead of time. Without Shan's knowledge, I had the legal documents prepared, and had my salary deposited into a new account. I had asked for his name to be removed from all my credit cards on December 1. These preparations would help me retain my bearings. They would hold me like a strong anchor.

A few days earlier, I had informed a couple, Rena and Neel, who were our friends, about my decision. These were fairly new friends that Shan had made. We played cards Friday evenings, a pastime I disliked immensely but with which I went along because Shan insisted. I went over to them and told Rena I was getting separated. She was horrified and told me that I was making the wrong decision.

"This kind of thing happens in every marriage, Rita, these are just small things."

"How do *you* know what I have gone through?"

My instinct for survival was so strong now that I bluntly added, "If you can't be a friend now, then talk to me after I have freed myself. I wanted to let you know because I thought you were someone I could turn to in case of an emergency."

She repeated what she had said. I was so angry that I banged the kitchen counter with my fist and stomped out of her house.

When I got in the car, I cried my heart out. It seemed as if I was going to be on my own. I expected I would get the same reaction from many women. This was not due to their friendship but to years of traditional conditioning.

I also did not seek help from my sister. She had a large family. If I could have involved only her, I would have gone to her. But I did not want other people to try to talk me out of the divorce.

There was no cloud of guilt around me, and I was not feeling vulnerable and weak. But, in spite of all I had gone through, I could not help feeling for Shan's suffering and his loss—his loss of me, and the collapse of his entire world. But it was too late to turn back; it had been too late for us a long time ago.

Many minutes passed that Sunday morning as we sat in the family room downstairs. It was ten o'clock, the children had eaten their breakfast and were waiting in the living room, doing their homework. Shan, sitting in his favorite spot on the couch, was watching TV, and I sat on another couch at the other end of the room, near the window. The rose curtain was open and the warm sunshine was coming through. I was glad for that small gesture from nature. In my mind I rehearsed my opening for the hundredth time, waiting for the right moment, the quiet moment on TV. And then, with the entire morning lying like a lump in my throat, the time came to perform. The world ground to a halt.

"I don't want to stay in this marriage." I told Shan, not very loudly, from across the room. I did not want a drama or a discussion, and I held out the document—the divorce papers—toward him. My outstretched hand trembled. I did not get up from my seat, but looked at him, waiting for his reaction.

Shan turned his head to look at me.

"I don't want to stay in this marriage," I repeated a little louder.

He turned the volume on the TV down with the remote control in his hand. He got up, in slow motion, and came toward me, and the look on his face gave way from blank expression to one of disbelief. He looked confused and it seemed as if I could feel his heart starting to pound.

Bending down to reach them, he took the papers from me to see what they were. There was shock on his face, as if he could not believe that I had gone so far as to generate the paperwork for a divorce.

"Why? What is wrong?" he asked softly. "I didn't know ... you wanted to leave."

I thought to myself, how could all this be news to him? I had threatened him about leaving many times, but he had chosen to ignore the warnings. And he knew that the last few months he had hardly been home.

Here *I* was, taken aback by his reaction.

Defending my actions would have left me open to having to justify my position. I did not want an argument. I was not negotiating for a better married life; I wanted to end it once and for all. There was no other way except to keep quiet and hope that he understood the seriousness and the finality of the decision. I was anxious, nervous, and the strain of telling him weighed like a dead tree trunk on my chest.

"I cannot stay in this relationship any longer. I want you, please, to sign the documents and leave me alone."

"Why didn't you tell me earlier that you were *that* unhappy? I would have tried to do something about it."

He said he would change, said all the things he had said to me a thousand times before. This is what I had wanted to avoid. I kept my end of the bargain to myself. I heard but I was not listening. My silence said it all.

"Please, give me one more chance, and I'll change everything. You'll see, please Munni, let's try and work it out."

I was not even sure he knew what he needed to change.

I hated to see him lose control. He looked so pathetic.

"I know I haven't been home, and I haven't paid attention to you or the children. I know all the things I have been doing wrong, but please give me time to turn things around," he pleaded. "I don't want these papers, please put them away...You have to give me a chance, babe...please."

A pause.

"I don't want a divorce."

A pause.

"Just one more chance, you'll see that I can change everything."

I listened to him. I felt sorry for him. He could not see the pity behind the deliberately blank expression on my face. In my heart I wanted to give him a break. Maybe he needed more time to absorb the fact that I was leaving him. He was obviously distraught beyond belief. I did care for him in my own odd way.

His reaction was different from the one I had expected. It would have been easier to leave an angry husband—easier to justify and easier to move away. But this soft-spoken person managed to twist some part of my spirit.

He stayed there in front of me for an hour, two hours.

I got up and went to the kitchen to get lunch for the kids. I was glad I could do that, even during an argument.

He followed me and pleaded, "Please, why don't you give me a chance? I will really change. And we can build a life together again."

"No," I insisted. "I've already prepared the papers."

"Please try to understand, Munni. I can't leave. I can't leave you and the kids. My life will be nothing. Please let us try to work this out nicely." He was crying. It was apparent that it had not even occurred to him that I would ever dream of leaving him.

More than half the day passed this way. I knew eventually he could make matters difficult for me. Right then he was pleading with me but there was no guarantee he would not become angry and heated, given time.

The way the day had played itself out, his reaction being nonviolent and pathetic made me feel sorry for him—because I knew that there was no one he could turn to. He was far too proud about his standing in society to seek help. Maybe he needed time to adjust—maybe I had been unfair to drop the news on him like a bomb. And separation was an option that would serve both our purposes, though I knew that a restraining order might be needed later. But I had to give him time to adjust, I felt, time to let the shock of my decision sink in.

"Perhaps," I said, "perhaps I'll talk to the lawyer to see how a separation could work."

In relenting once again, though not completely, in showing consideration for him, perhaps I was revealing my weaker side again. But again, I don't know what the outcome would have been otherwise.

"Please move out of the house today. The children need me, and they need the house," I said patiently.

After several hours, in the late evening, he honored this request, taking almost nothing with him. Before leaving, he said:

"I want to see Nina and Vi everyday—I'll be lost without them. I can't live without seeing them. Can I come straight from work and see them?"

He was treading softly, not wanting to displease me.

"All right," I replied.

Shan walked out the door sad, dejected, and very alone. I had no idea where he was going or what he would do. It was now evening and the darkness was starting to descend. I closed the door behind him. He didn't say goodbye to the children. They had been quiet throughout the day and gone about their work.

I hugged them at length, and we talked about Dad—they wondered where he would go. We were all in a pensive and subdued state, with mixed feelings, but glad that the ordeal was finally over.

A state of shock lingered around me the next day. And the next. Shan's moving away felt strange: like a death in the family. I did not feel happy and I wished that he had been less angry, less jealous, less manipulative, and less secretive so that we could have led a normal life. I hated him for his condescending and unwarranted behavior towards me and the children. There was nothing cheerful about this new freedom. But now, at least, I would not have to watch carefully my every word, my every action. I would not have to ask permission, I would not have to negotiate silly little things. I could make friends and talk to people without fear of him listening to my conversations. I could manage my own finances.

It took every ounce of strength not to let pathos and softness invade my determination.

In time, after a few days, a wholesome relief fell from the skies and uplifted my soul, freeing it from the impressions of my dark past and from feelings of emptiness and guilt. I could have lain down on the grass and stretched my limbs to embrace the warm earth, the sky, and the deep blue horizon.

Downhill

What actually followed were six months of agony, every day a test of patience and courage. No one could have anticipated the turn of events that happened. What I had expected to be peaceful days ahead for me turned out to be chaotic and turbulent. I was subject to Shan's protests, his silently hostile demonstrations, and the insistence that he return to my home, my life.

The pain of separation was too raw for him and he needed the strength and security of hearth and home. He came straight home from work, saying he could not live without the children. His worried face spoke of his desperate existence. I took pity on him but kept to myself and carried on with the tasks at hand. He ate whatever I cooked, but his appetite had shrunk. He must have had a burning hope that we would live together "normally" again, but I was careful not to fan it. I don't think he knew what to do with himself. He seemed to be in some kind of trance, blindly responding to his immediate surroundings. Usually he stayed until midnight, not wanting to leave the place he thought was his home.

I felt for his loss and would have felt it all the more had he not followed me around the house in a pseudohypnotic state, watching me intently, desolately. What happened to all his going out after work and his late nights? He had offered no explanation for his conduct in the previous months. I felt an underlying menace, though, lurking in his quiet behavior. I pitied him to the point that, ordinarily, I would have accepted him back. But now I was passionate in my resolve and determined to see myself through to sanity and happiness. After a lifetime of fluctuating hope and deception, I felt I deserved my freedom.

When I returned home after work, Shan would already be there. From the minute I stepped inside the house, he followed me. He followed me to my bedroom, where I first went to change into my casual clothes. He stood outside the door if I closed it. If I didn't, he came inside and watched whatever I did—changing the sheets, finding an old bill, putting laundry away. When I went downstairs and sat with the children, he came and sat near us and watched me help them with homework, or read the school communiqués, or talk to Vijay and Nina regarding their activities. He watched me unpack their lunch boxes and get dinner ready. He ate with us and then watched me as I cleaned up the table and washed the dishes, all the while not saying a word. We did not include him in the conversations, but at the same time we could not tell him to go away. Many times I told him he had to leave, but he constantly said, "I can't live without the children." He stayed home and watched TV if I went for groceries; if I took Vijay for swimming or skating, he followed us in his car and sat nearby, watching. After the children were settled, I sat in the family or dining room with my office work and my laptop. He watched me, and now that I was alone he would say, "Please take me back, Munni."

The place he had rented increased his dejection. It was a semi-finished basement apartment very close to where we lived. I don't know whether he couldn't afford a decent place, or whether he was in the mood for self-deprivation, or whether he did not want to be far from us, but his dismal accommodation contributed deeply to his already neurotic state.

I asked him to see a doctor or a therapist, although I knew that he would not do so. He had always preferred to keep away from them. He did not think anything was wrong with him. If we just got back together, he said, he would be all right. He had never wanted me to go to doctors either. "They will find something wrong with you," he would say. "It's better not to go." I had had to fight to see a dentist, and it was many years before he allowed me to go for physical check-ups.

But now he wanted me and the family back. He asked me to go with him to a marriage counselor. I refused.

He began to lose weight and suffered from what I would learn later was sheer depression. He became more and more subdued and was starting to lose all sense of normality.

As the weeks wore on, his following me around became obsessive. I felt as if a tormented ghost were hovering around me, penetrating me with wide unblinking eyes and silent looks. When he walked, his head hung low, as he stared indifferently at the ground under his feet. And he would utter: "Please, Munni, please, please take me back."

The children were in the same predicament as I, though their plight was perhaps worse because they did not know how to deal with it. They were unnerved by his pacing, his intent watchfulness, and they complained to me. Shan would stand at the doorway of their room, staring at them for minutes on end, while they listened to music, or talked to their friends on the phone, or worked on the computer, or played Nintendo. They could only ignore him, they did not love him enough to feel sorry for him. They wanted him to go away and stop menacing them. But they were too polite to shut the door on him. Perhaps a restraining order would have eased our situation, but there was no telling, it might have infuriated him, a chance I could not afford to take. I wanted to make sure that there was no possibility of violence. He had never been violent with the children, and I did not want this to change. Thus there was no choice but to try and solve the problem in a peaceful way. He stayed in the evenings until finally I told him he just had to leave. Most days it would be past eleven.

One evening, he entered Nina's room. She was sitting at her desk doing school work. Standing at the doorway, he begged, "Please love me, please take me back." What can a sixteen-year-old do when a father implores her for love? It wasn't so much that she did not care, as that she was caught between her own feelings of revulsion and sympathy. The children's emotions of love, hate, pity, anger, and frustration were wrapped up in a ball of outward composure, which they had no hope of untangling in the current circumstances. Nina did not want him there, she wanted him to stop coming to the house; and if he came, then to behave in a way that was not embarrassing. I think we all would have tolerated him if he had behaved normally.

In hindsight, perhaps I should have been harder on him and told him to stay away completely. But I believed then, and do so now, that restricting him from coming home would have had an even worse effect on him and us. He might have stalked me, or come to work and made a scene, or gone to the children's school and embarrassed them. All these were real possibilities. He might even have become violent with me and harmed me, or tied me up, or locked me up, or scared the wits out of me by threatening me with what he could do with the kids. The worst he could have done, I thought, was to take away Vijay forcibly after school and run away to India. Nina was too old for that, but Vijay was frightened of him and it would have been easy to coerce the child into doing anything. Vijay was always the more frightened child: he would sleep with lights on, he would wet his bed at night, he would want to be near me. Many nights he would walk into my bedroom and sleep on the floor with Nina's old RainbowBrite blanket, on a mattress that was permanently on the floor for his use.

The separation agreement split everything fairly, except that I would hold on to the mortgaged house and make its payments, due to the proximity of the children's school. When we started discussing the division, he challenged me on every count, and I realized that he was not interested in making the process work. He wanted what he wanted, as always.

I revised my offer to suit him. We came down from eleven points in the agreement to seven. I gave up the conditions demanding that we split certain of our items and told him that I would accommodate whatever he wished. I was desperate to come to an agreement, I had convinced myself that I would do so even if I lost everything except the kids. Every week the document would be redrafted and every week he would reject it. Finally I gave in to everything, except that I would continue to live in the house and make its payments and the children would stay with me. It was the maximum I could give. He rejected this offer too.

Our finances were far from stable. His debts were guaranteed by the house, and so they could also become my liability. But he never disclosed the extent of those debts.

"How much do you owe them?" I would ask.

"It depends. Munni, can't we get back together please?"

He dug in his heels and refused to cooperate with anything. And so we never officially separated.

No End in Sight

"I have to move back into the house," he said to me one weekend toward the end of March. "It is so depressing in that basement. I can't concentrate at work," he continued, looking gloomy and forlorn. "If I stay there any longer I'll go crazy."

The basement was not finished. He had to hang his shirts on two-by-fours; the walls and floor were concrete. His room was right next to the furnace, but he was always cold.

"I am really afraid of losing my job," he said.

I knew that he couldn't afford much. The room was costing him three hundred dollars a month. Most of his money probably went towards paying the debts.

I looked at him—at the frustration on his face, his thin body, his shrinking frame. How he was living in that semi-dungeon was unimaginable. I was afraid that if he lost his job it would be harder on everyone, for I would have to support him and I was stretched financially. I was sentimental and soft, too much the Indian woman: I did not want to see him ruined. All I wanted was for him to leave me alone.

So he moved into the guest bedroom, the farthest one from mine.

What transpired was worse than I had imagined, and perhaps many people would say, rightly so.

At five a.m., he would open the door, enter my bedroom, and kneeling by the side of the bed, shake me and whisper:

"Munni? Munni! Wake up!"

He would be peering at me.

"You can't wake me up now! Go away!" I would say half asleep, not wanting to wake Vijay, who was sleeping next to me.

"Please, Munni, please listen to me…"

Vijay slept with me because he was afraid of his father; I also felt safe in his presence. Sometimes he would remain fast asleep when Shan came, but at other times Vijay woke up. He pretended to be asleep but listened to the goings on and he would hug me or move closer after Shan left. He would say, "I wish Dad wouldn't trouble you," or "Maybe we can go away somewhere where he can't find us."

"Yes, Vijay," I would answer. "Soon we'll be fine."

Shan's weird behavior should have warned me. He was evidently unstable and probably dangerous. But I had lived with him so long, had seen so much of his irrational, compulsive, and selfish ways, and also, at present, I felt so confident in my freedom that I was blinded to just how dangerous and unpredictable he could be.

Scared to Death

One weekday morning, while I was packing the school lunches, Shan started an upbeat conversation, telling me how he would make sure that everything would be different from before, and I should have no fear about getting back together with him.

Nina and Vi left for school, kissing me good-bye.

My mind was a million miles away. I was in a rush to go to work, knowing I had a hectic schedule that day. As I started for the garage door, the entrance to which was from the laundry room at the side of the house, he moved in front of me and blocked my path.

"Listen to me! I can't wait any longer! How much longer do you want me wait?"

He stood before me, hands stretched out wide against the white door behind him, to prevent me from leaving.

"Please move, I have to leave for work," I said, trying to sound patient, which I didn't feel. I was angry.

Suddenly he started swearing at me, using the most offensive language.

"Bitch! Whore! You'll never get away with this! What the fuck, do you think you can just *leave* me? You think I'll just let you go? Stupid bitch!"

His face was contorted with fury; he looked dreadful in his jogging pants and his navy T-shirt, his favorite attire.

He was still spewing out filth when I tried to make a dash past him. But he was solid of form and athletic, and I could not get an inch past him. He pushed me away, and I bounced against the washing machine, quite shaken up.

"Move!" I shouted at him.

"Listen to me, bitch! Whore…"

"Leave me alone! Let me go!" I was yelling to be let out and he was shouting to be taken back. I was crying and gulping air.

It infuriated him that the loudness of his voice did not wield the power it once did. So he shouted louder and wiggled his finger at me. With clenched teeth, he said: "I will never, never let you go!"

It had not occurred to me to call the police. But he would have run and snatched the phone from me anyway. We carried on this way for half an hour. His rage would be interspersed with pathetic pleas. At my wits' end, I started walking around, like a hunted animal, he watching my every move like a wild and impatient hunter.

Suddenly there was a knock. Shan went to open the front door. There was a man standing there, saying something about a broken fence.

I took my chance and walked hastily from the kitchen into the laundry room. As I entered the garage, Shan came running after me again. I got into the van, through the small passage between the door and the garage wall. As I started the vehicle, Shan opened my door, and started pleading again. I had the urge simply to reverse so that he would be forced to move. I began to do that ever so slowly. I did not want to harm him, but I did want badly to run away as far as possible from this madman. He did not budge until eventually I stepped on the gas and he had no choice but to get out of the way.

There were tears rolling down my face and my body was trembling. I felt I never wanted to go into the house again. I did not know where I was headed. I could not possibly go to work. It was about 10:30 a.m., the whole scene must have taken well over an hour and a half. I drove and I drove.

I was alienated from friends and family and was unsure where to go. Having isolated myself, there was no one to turn to. That is the downside of having become fiercely independent. But I ended up going to a friend, Ranju, whose children were friends of Vijay and Nina.

I never wanted to face an incident like that again, and I was not sure how I was going to manage my life.

The Sunday Before: Premonitions

Finally I told Shan to move out of the house again and pressured him to find a place of his own.

A few days after I gave him notice he unexpectedly said: "Can you come with me to look for a place? I don't know anything about looking for apartments."

A breakthrough! Finally he was beginning to understand that we *were* supposed to be separated. Just because I could never get past the legal issue of him not signing the documents didn't mean that I didn't *feel* separated. It was a Sunday morning. He wanted us to go that very afternoon and I agreed. I would have done anything to be rid of him, even if it meant helping him in the process.

"Do you have some addresses that we can follow up on?" I asked.

"I just want to check out some areas around Don Mills and Sheppard. Sometimes they have vacancy signs outside the apartment complexes."

In an instant, my elation evaporated. I thought to myself that he couldn't be serious about looking for a place at all. Nevertheless, I left Nina and Vi to take care of themselves and went apartment hunting with Shan. He was driving his red Toyota Corolla. After some ten minutes, I suddenly realized he was heading in the opposite direction, north. We drove north on McCowan Road, past Highway 16 where the residential area stopped, past Major Mackenzie. I was suddenly very scared. My heart started pounding. Alarmed, I asked him why he was taking this route.

"There will be traffic the other way, so I thought we would go this way."

"On a Sunday afternoon?" This was definitely not a good sign.

Where was he taking me? We were in the middle of nowhere, not a soul in sight, just one farm after another.

Suddenly, he stopped by the roadside, the car kicked up a load of gravel and dust. There were brown fields all around us dotted with a few evergreens. And there was a sinking feeling in the pit of my stomach. I had a horrific image of being cut up into pieces and thrown away in the woods.

The only weapon I had was the bunch of keys I was clutching in my right fist, away from his sight. I held the largest one in a strong grip and wished desperately I had control of the steering wheel.

"Why are we stopping here?"

Perhaps he was aware of my panic; he certainly was aware of my suspicions.

He said softly, "I just want to talk to you."

I told him he could talk to me somewhere else, not there and not then. Right then we wanted to look for a place for him to live.

He turned around and we left for Don Mills and Sheppard.

We drove by a blue-green glass-covered high-rise at normal speed, took a few pretentious rounds, and his "hunting" was complete. Not once did we get out of the car to inquire for an apartment. To this day, when I go past that particular building at Don Mills and York Mills, I can think of nothing else but his erratic behavior, and I am reminded of that sinking feeling I experienced in the car.

On the way back, he stopped at the local plaza and talked for more than a hour in the car. I was averse to car conversations for obvious reasons. I felt helpless and cornered. He was trying to win me back by pleading with me, except this time his pleas were not quite so emotional. He was trying to persuade me logically and trying to understand how flexible I was.

That night I called a different lawyer, David, and told him I did not know what to do, I needed legal guidance and sound advice. What were my options if my spouse refused to sign any agreements? Could I get a divorce anyway or did he *have* to consent? I told David we should meet, and I set up an appointment with him.

The weather was warming and little green buds colored the trees lime green. The magnolias were blooming in the front lawn. The kids were once again on the street riding their bikes or rollerblading. Vijay would hang around with Scott or Christopher or Matthew, mostly involved in band or sports. He was a big boy who dared to ride his bike down a flight of stairs, who could glide along ice with grace and could jump on his roller blades over concrete edges. He was also an easy child who could keep himself amused with any of a dozen activities. What a sense of humor he had! He would clown around at home and I later learnt that he did the same at school. I remember once how when he was two or three years old he had asked for a 7-Up, calling it "senen-up." Amused, I repeatedly tried to make him say the name correctly. Finally, tired of my antics, he said exasperatedly but resourcefully, "Okay, mama, give me ginger ale!"

Tuesday

Spring tried to cheer me up, but I was running ragged, feeling depleted day by day. Vijay's birthday was coming up and we had planned to take his friends for a wavepool party. Vi was excited, and we went to the mall to get his haircut and buy cake decorations. I asked Shan to take him to the barber but he refused. Nina did not want to stay behind with Dad, so she came with Vijay and me to the mall. As we walked into the building from the parking lot, we saw Shan some ten paces behind us. Vi and I walked on towards our destination, but Nina stayed behind to confront her Dad. I could not hear anything but knew that she was criticizing his behavior right there in the midst of the crowds around us. I had not expected her to take such a stand openly, though recently she had started to hold her own and talked back to Dad. She was a new force that Shan had to contend with. I felt proud and knew that I should have shed my subservient role a long time ago—if only for her, to be the right role model for her.

I was bringing work home every day and burning the midnight oil. I was free to pursue what I wanted, no one now controlled what I did or where I went. I had a new desire to learn, to know everything, to start my own business. I wished to make something of myself.

Thursday: My Life Burns Down

Thursday morning the same week, I was surprised that Shan did not force upon me his usual obsessive pleas about getting back together. In fact, he had not done so the night before either. Now, while making sandwiches for school, I saw him walk into the kitchen to join me, still in his Adidas jogging pants. He hung around, not saying a word. He was certainly in one of his more subdued states. I told him I would be coming home late—there was a five o'clock meeting that probably would go on till seven or eight. I asked him to please look after the kids if they needed anything.

As luck would have it, my meeting was cancelled, but I had to deliver my report for four at a location not far from home. Good, I thought, I can take Nina to the optometrist. I had had to cancel the appointment earlier. Shan had never taken any of the kids for their appointments, and I did not ask him this time.

I reached home at 4:15. Vijay was boisterously playing his drums, happily waiting for me to arrive home. The kids tried to ignore Dad as much as possible. I dashed upstairs to change into my casuals, and the kids came in the bedroom to hang around with me. They were playful, watching some inconsequential clips on TV while we talked, all at the same time, all sitting on the bed. I told Nina to get ready, we were going to see Dr Peters after all. The appointment was for 5:30. I had to pick up something from the mall too, so could we please leave a little early.

Shan walked up to the bedroom just then, surprising me.

"I thought you were at work," I said.

"I had an upset stomach so I called in sick today," he replied. I had no reason to doubt him.

He stood still at the doorway, looking vacant and subdued, half observing the three of us, half engrossed in his own world. His shirt and pants hung loose on him. The kids became quiet.

"Come on, Nina, lets go," I jumped up from the bed.

"How long will you be?" Shan asked quietly.

"About an hour or so, I think."

"Can I come too, Mom?" Vijay asked.

"I'll take you to the mall in a while," his Dad replied before I had a chance to think.

I went past Shan and out of the bedroom.

"Then can I buy a pair of jeans, Mom?" Vijay called out, coming out of the room behind me.

I was half way down the stairs, attempting to make up for lost time.

"Sure, go ahead!" I said, looking up at him from the bottom of the stairs.

"How about two jeans?" he asked cheekily, and grinned from ear to ear, leaning on the upstairs railing in the foyer.

"Whatever you want, Vi," I replied lightly, knowing he would do no such thing. I walked out to the garage with Nina.

As always, it was a long wait at Dr Peters. Nina wanted colored contacts and we tried this pair and that with the help of a friendly assistant whom we had come to know over the course of several years. Finally finished at 6:30 or so, we headed back home.

It was a short drive, and just three or four houses before we reached home, we saw people dashing along on the pavement in the same direction as us. I didn't recognize them, but they saw us, and began shouting at us, and flagging at us. A shiver ran down my spine.

"Fire! There's a fire at the back of your house…someone's called 911…"

Unexpected Events

I ran to the back of the house, past the wooden fence. Oh my God! Oh my God! Where's Vijay? Where's Shan? They should be out here, where *are* they? Maybe at the mall, hopefully at the mall!

Inside, the rose-colored curtains of the family room are drawn, but I see huge orange flames licking the sides of the drapes. I know for sure that Shan and Vi are inside. The flames have already reached the ceiling of the family room. There is no smoke outside the house, but inside the fire is devouring everything as fast as it can, and crackling so fiercely I can hear it. Vijay, Shan, where are they, I ask myself again and again. Quickly, I pick up the long wooden veranda broom lying next to the barbecue cylinder outside the glass doors. I hold it poised, ready to smash windows and doors. I *have* to get inside. I *have* to let the fire out.

Leave them alone, Fire.

I am about to swing the broom handle. A fireman comes rushing up to me out of nowhere. I had not even heard the fire trucks coming. He tugs the broom away from my hand, yelling, "Go to the front of the house…*now!*"

"There are two people inside!" I scream back at him. "Can you hear me?"

You have a gas mask on, how can you possibly hear me, I think. The fire is deafening.

I shout from the top of my lungs: "There are two people inside!"

I go to the front, round the side of the house, and peer in through the garage window on the way to see if the red vehicle is in the garage. Yes, I see the vague red shape of Shan's Toyota. So they are inside, they didn't go to the mall after all…

"Nina, come here! Can you see the red car? Is it really there?" I ask her hurriedly as she comes running.

Peering in, she nods, "Oh my God. I think so!"

A couple of Nina's friends are already on the scene. Someone has moved the van from the driveway to the roadside. The noise of the sirens is loud, as more engines arrive at the scene. The neighborhood has filled up with fire trucks, police cars, and crowds.

I stand on the pavement by myself, watching the firefighters, anxious for Vi. Maybe I'll see him on his bike—he always rides his bike in the evenings. If I am lucky, he will ride up to me and ask what happened. He'll come soon—I'm sure he's somewhere here.

One of Vi's childhood babysitters, Jill, comes up to me and asks me if there is anything she can do to help.

Come on, Vi, please come to me from *somewhere.* Come to your Mom.

The fire fighters are trying to get into the house, but for some reason they can't. I try yelling at them from a distance. There are two people inside! Do they hear me, do they know? They are too busy trying to put out the fire. Nobody has even asked me if I *live* here.

Why are Shan or Vi not poking their heads out of a window? Why are they not screaming for help? Surely they can get to a window. Why haven't they got to a window? First floor, second floor, basement. The fire has not eaten up the whole house – look, the front of the house is still standing, is so calm. How could they be trapped inside?

Where's Nina? I can't see where she is—there are so many people.

There is a clearing in the crowd where I am standing.

A police officer asks me to go and stand by one of their cars across the road. I go reluctantly, not wanting to be so far away. Ambulances have arrived, stand unobtrusively some five hundred feet to the left of me. There is a radius of fifty feet around me, in which stands nothing but the white police car. I lean on the hood. I am in a daze. I wait for Vi to show up on his bike. I know that it is only a wish. Please, God, let them be okay.

It will just be a matter of minutes. They are trapped inside. The firemen will get them out.

But time passes, ticking ever so slowly. I am not myself—this alien feeling. I am suspended in some unseen and timeless whirl. My inert body is a heavy burden. Everything is slow motion. I can hear a buzz around me. More time passes. Each precious moment passes. My heart sinks lower and lower. Hope is dwindling fast, fast, fast, into an endless abyss. I am painfully aware of the news awaiting me.

"Miss, we can't find anyone in the house," a policeman says, coming towards me. His black cap is still on his head, that's a good sign.

"Do you know where they might be?" he asks me.

Hope flickers again.

"Maybe in the family room, at the back to the left, or in the master bedroom, upstairs right, at the back," I say, pointing this way and that, anxious to be understood.

He walks back, too slowly. Why isn't he rushing?

They can't find anyone. Perhaps Vi and Shan went to the mall after all. But the car in the garage is a dead giveaway. I am only deluding myself.

No one comes out.

I change my plea to *Bhagwaan*: "Please, only keep them alive if they are okay. If they are burnt badly, please God—don't make them suffer."

The firefighters bring out something from the house. I can't see what they are doing—the shrubbery is in the way, and the magnolia tree too. I don't walk up to peer. Something inside me senses defeat. Two policemen are standing nearby. The firefighters roll a stretcher towards the ambulance, coming across the road but going diagonally, away from me. I can see Shan's foot—a sock half fallen off. The foot is clean, fair and unblemished. No burns. The rest of him is covered in a white sheet. They are taking him to the ambulance, so he must be alive. I don't notice that the ambulance just sits there, does not roar away with its recent occupant, its urgent siren blaring.

Now they take something else out, and also roll it on a stretcher to the ambulance. No one is with me. I am aware of the crowds moving about nearby, starting to disperse. It is a movie. This is not my life, my family, but some live drama.

"Miss, do you have any close relatives or friends here?" Does he still have his cap on? Yes he does.

No, I shake my head, not here right now.

I wonder why he is asking. Does he want to tell me something? But he's thinking I cannot take it, so he's not going to tell me anything now. I don't press him.

"We should go to the hospital now," continues this kind young policeman.

We drive off in the police car. It is the first time I have been in one.

"Do you think they are okay?" I ask.

He says, "I don't really know. I hope so."

We drive pretty much in silence. I feel like a little girl, so helpless in what seems to be a huge seat.

Devastated

We headed to an emergency room of the hospital, and I was asked to sit in a small room. Mark, the policeman, left the door open and stood by it. The phone in the room stared at me. I picked it up and called Didi. She said she would come and be with me immediately.

I called Raj in Detroit. Sweety, his wife, said that he had left for Toronto that day to attend a business meeting. He was staying in Markham, and I could contact him at his hotel.

I sat alone on the long green couch in the sparse, oblong-shaped waiting room. Mark excused himself.

From somewhere, Nina, her friend Seema, and Seema's father turned up. I had not seen him before. I can't remember if we spoke much. We sat together for a long time, or so it seemed. I had not paid any attention to Nina from the time we had driven up to the house. She was distressed and wanted answers.

Mark returned. He removed his cap and said, "I'm afraid they didn't make it."

"That's not true—go check again!" Nina exclaimed.

I looked at him blankly. My mind was empty and there was nothing to say. There was no sensation, no thought. Just an immense vacuum expanding into eternity.

My sister turned up and she hugged me.

"They didn't make it," I told her blankly. "I don't know what happened, how it happened."

We were escorted to another waiting room, just my sister and I. Nina was taken elsewhere—to be questioned separately, I believe.

There were three or four policemen in the second waiting room. One of them said, "I'm detective so-and-so, and I will be in charge of this investigation. We'd like to take a statement from you. Can you tell us everything that happened leading up to the event?"

I wanted badly to know what had happened, but at the same time I was afraid of knowing.

I spoke quietly, as though I didn't want people to hear my thoughts—the separation, the fights, and all that. I told them that I didn't think I had left the iron on, or the stove on. Perhaps, for once, I thought to myself, Shan had been trying his hand at cooking, and he could have left the stove on. I told the detective I couldn't imagine what could have started the fire. It must have taken well over an hour to get through my story: yes, we had had some violence before; no I never charged him; no, I hadn't noticed anything strange about him today except that he seemed very subdued; no I did not have a fight with him today; yes, Vijay got along with him, but he was a little frightened of him too. I answered their questions readily, with ease, there was nothing to hide. One of them was busy scribbling notes.

The thought that I would never see Vijay again had not clearly registered in my mind. When it occurred, fleetingly, I dismissed it as insane and unreal. How could that be? It was ridiculous. It was impossible.

In some ways I still believe that. In some very subtle and faraway part of the mind you expect that they will return. Sometime in the future. Somehow. By some magic or miracle. The harshness of the concrete world is exactly that; it does not live in harmony with that part of the mind which hopes and simply believes.

Finally, after the interview, I was told that the coroner would come and talk to me.

"What is a coroner?" I asked.

"The person who has to legally pronounce them dead," said the chief detective.

It was now about 9:30 p.m. I did not wonder about Nina, or anybody or anything, for that matter. There was probably no expression on my face and I felt nothing.

Somebody was needed to identify the bodies. I wanted to see Vi but Didi stopped me. "You should remember him as he was," she said. I wanted to know how badly burnt they were, whether they suffered much. Besides, I couldn't change my mind afterwards—this would be a final decision. I let the thought go. Maybe they were right, I wouldn't be able to handle the image of their burnt bodies afterwards.

The coroner, a Dr Maclean from the Trauma Unit of Sunnybrook Hospital, walked into the waiting room and sat down on the couch opposite me. Under any other circumstances he would have seemed an amiable, sincere, and caring man. To the right of him was the scribbling detective of before.

"This wasn't a natural death," the detective said, his head low-ered, looking up at me with raised eyebrows.

"What do you mean?" I replied, truly not understanding his statement.

When he didn't reply, the coroner took over.

"We found your son's throat cut. The cut was made by a knife."

"What?…How?…tell me… "

When I insisted on knowing, he took his hand to his own throat, ran a finger across it, showing me how long the cut was. From ear to ear, almost. The coroner did not mean to be cruel; he was being exact and graphic.

There are no words to describe my thoughts.

My mind was suddenly a slashed high voltage wire, swinging wildly back and forth. I was afraid for Vijay. So very afraid.

Did he torture him? I thought, when I regained my senses. How much, what *did* he do? I thought about him being cut up into pieces, his limbs cut off.

I don't think I had moved a muscle. Can a storm brew in a chest that upholds an expressionless face?

"What else, did you find anything else?" I asked the coroner.

"No, there were no other wounds."

"How did the fire start?"

"We are investigating, but it looks like your husband set himself on fire."

"How long would it have taken for Vijay to die?"

"Instantaneously," the coroner said. "There is a vein in the neck around here," he pointed to a place on his own neck. "When punctured, the person dies immediately."

He added, after a pause, "We think your son died before the fire started—he does not have as many burns on his body. Both the bodies were found in the furnace room of the basement."

Although I wanted to know all the details, it was difficult enough to grasp and accept what I had just learned. I was trying to swallow the flood in one gulp.

Nina was called in, and she sat at the edge of the seat between Didi and me.

"Do you want to know how Vi died?" I said without thinking.

She stared at me wide eyed, then looked at the coroner.

The coroner said softly, "We found a knife next to your brother."

Before he could begin the next sentence, she jumped up, screaming, "Nooooooo...I hate him!..."

She burst into tears and bolted out of the room.

I have no idea how many minutes passed before Dr Maclean said he would need to conduct an autopsy to determine the exact cause of death.

When I came out of the waiting room and into the main reception area, I saw hordes of people—Nina's friends, Nina's teachers, Vijay's school principal, officials. I spoke to Nina. She said she was going to stay with her friends, was that okay. I was in no shape or form to look after her, so I was thankful to those who were with her. I had no idea how much everyone else knew—I assumed they knew very little, only that both the father and son had died.

We were finally done by about midnight. My friend Ranju, whose office I had run to a few weeks ago, came to my rescue at the hospital and took me to her home.

We stopped at my brother's hotel on the way. Raj, who had

wanted to come to the hospital, had been told by Didi to wait, we were going to be done at the hospital very shortly. Raj seldom came to Toronto for business, for him to be here for me was surely the intervention of providence. Every little action is a function of the great wheel of life, I believe. But my brother's visit was not the only coincidence. That day the full moon was out, and it was a Thursday as well. For me, Thursday is the most auspicious day of the week, and Buddh Poornima is one of the most significant full-moon days for a Hindu. Vijay was divinely blessed in his parting from the world. I could take solace in this.

I was exhausted and fell asleep instantly, only to wake up at what must have been three a.m. I wondered whether I had been in a nightmare. It felt as if real life were pulsating in a dream world, and I was disoriented. What was reality and what was not? I noticed the strange bed and my borrowed clothing and came to realize that truly my Vi was gone. My head on the pillow, I stared and stared at the twinkling lights of the city, visible outside the ninth-story apartment. It felt so strange. Slowly I realized that I must have lost everything I possessed to the fire: my house, all my personal belongings, everything that I ever owned. But that was nothing. Nothing compared to losing Vijay. But these were words. I could not *feel* anything. There was a void in my mind and in my heart; there was a void around me. And the void filled itself with more void. The vacant space in front of me was devoid of emotion and ripples of vacuum were encircling in larger orbits. This is what it would feel like if I ever got lost in space and was destined to float around forever. It was a world where there was no air to breathe and the silence was deafening, and one had no hope of ever reaching any destination.

Six

The Aftermath

The Devastation: Reliving the Agony

While I had been sitting in the waiting room at the hospital late into the night, news of the tragedy had been broadcast to the world, and it knew more than I did. The nine o'clock evening news called the event a "murder-suicide." The phrase had not occurred to me. It seemed cruel and insensitive; sadly incomplete. No one reading the newspapers or listening to the news could possibly have any idea of what lay behind the deaths of my son and husband, and therefore the term "murder-suicide" seemed foreign.

The events that may have caused Vijay to suffer were tormenting my mind, and I was driven to seek out details. Did he have to fight back? Was he frightened beyond what his little heart could take? Perhaps if I could piece together how it happened, I would also know why it happened. Was it an accident-in-time, was it a fight between Dad and child that triggered the event? If Shan was devastated, he could have taken himself, but why take an innocent life? And that of his own son? What was going through his mind? Was the *murder-suicide* premeditated? If so, how long had it been on his mind? Was it me he was really after?

The next day the police wanted me to go with them into the house.

"We'd like you to remove any valuables, since we have to board up the house. You can come again later to take out other things that you may need, but for now, if there are any documents or jewelry, please remove them."

Two police officers came with me, holding large flashlights. They had provided me with overalls, to keep the soot off my clothes. I had put them on inside the police trailer which was parked in front of the house. A yellow band of tape went around the isolated trailer and part of the house, which we entered through the front door. Faint light came through the blackened windows and burnt-out shutters. Glass pieces from the shattered chandelier were strewn across the ceramic tiles, which were also covered with soot and small debris. The once beige curtains in the foyer were black. I smelt the smoke. I could see the two-by-four posts behind the broken drywall, ripped like paper here and there. Total devastation. Behind it lay the images of death, of Vi.

We had to walk over the rubble everywhere. The family room had a gaping hole in the floor made by the fire. It was this room that was in the worst shape. Shining through the darkness were the huge coiled springs of the couch, the distorted and twisted metal of the TV. There was very little of anything left: the fire had licked every scrap it possibly could. There was no trace of the computer or the desk it had lain on. The family videos had all evaporated into smoke. But on the brick above the fireplace were two ghastly strips of the shiny metal hands of the once-crimson clock, reading what seemed to be 6:27p.m. I closed my eyes briefly, imagining the horror behind the devastation.

In the kitchen, the ivory light fixture had fallen flat on the formerly cream-colored island counter and looked like a huge fried egg. The freezer door was open and twisted downward; some of its contents lay distorted and discolored on the floor. The roof in the kitchen had come apart and there was a ray of light peering perversely through. It should have turned away, nauseated. Most of the house was already boarded up and it looked like a scene from a yellowed black-and-white movie, with eerie sunlight shining through. The smell of burned charcoal was everywhere.

I was afraid to go up the stairs for fear of them giving way, but then I saw one of the detectives climb up and followed him. I turned into Vi's room, the first one at the top of the stairs. His Toronto Blue Jays sheets were dark with smoke, his altar statues blackened. His Nintendo, his CDs and his games were scattered on the floor, warped by the heat. The white bookshelf and the desk, along with all their contents were now a mass of gray and black. The drums he had played only yesterday and his jersey lay on the floor. I saw all this futile destruction, and finally I let the swell of tears roll down my face.

Shan had wanted me to suffer, this was clear. If he had had a chance, he would have taken Nina too. Perhaps he had intended that, but his plans had been spoiled by my coming home early. He had been true to the words he had used many times in the past: "You'll have to stay and suffer, won't you?"

I dragged the two-drawer metal chest out of my bedroom. It had most of the documents I would need. My hands blackened in no time. The place was hot, moist, and dark, except for the beam from my flashlight, which wavered here and there. The policeman took the file drawer downstairs.

I was still intent on learning how long Vijay had to bear his ordeal. The battery-operated alarm clock in the bedroom read 6:25, in agreement with the clock downstairs.

"I don't understand why everything was not burnt down by the fire," I said to the policeman who had come upstairs with me.

"Because all the doors and windows were locked from the inside, and when the oxygen inside the house was used up, the fire started dying out. That's why the firemen had a hell of a time determining how to get into the house. They didn't want the fire to spread either outside or inside the house."

So Shan had locked all the doors from the inside. The front, the garage, and the back doors were usually open in the evenings when the entire family was around.

It felt eerie to see everyday objects bent out of shape, *if* you could make out what they were. Everywhere lay blurry dark shapes, until you turned something over. Here were items I had used only yesterday morning—my rose-colored pillow, the white comb, my pearly nail polish, a shopping list, a pen.

I picked up some odd sentimental objects—some photos, my poetry books, my mother's jewelry—and walked out of the bedroom. The policeman told me I could come back later.

I went to the guest bedroom where Shan had been staying.

Were those his pants on the floor? I looked carefully, picked them up, and looked for the pockets. I found his wallet and gave it to the policeman.

Finally I stepped out of the house.

It was a dark world in there and it could consume you, pulling you towards utter devastation, its phantoms dragging you into a nether world of extinction and despair.

Was it possible for this to happen in an educated, professional family—in this century—in this materially advanced western hemisphere; to the most innocent of boys, who held no grudge, whose heart was so soft that he was afraid of the dark, of monsters, of scolding?

The television reporters, waiting outside the house, had decently left me alone.

I wanted to cry, but the tears would not come.

Byron came to a mind already spinning with disorientation:

As springs in deserts found seem sweet, all brackish though they be,
So midst the wither'd waste of life those tears would flow to me!

Raj went to fetch Nina the next day. Unable to help her, I had let her friends take care of her. She had been under the impression that Vijay had been tortured and had lived with the thoughts of a tormented brother for some time now. There was no room for consolation—she had to accept and come to terms with the bitter, cold truth. She had cried constantly. In the days to come, she would often say: "Why him, why not me?"

We went to the house again, along with the two detectives, Gary and Joe, who were assigned to my case.

I wanted to see the place where Vijay had died. I asked if we could go to the basement. It had a furnace room that doubled as a storeroom. It had been fairly well kept but filled to the brim with things—huge cardboard boxes, shelves with old cushions, strollers, suitcases, skates that were too small. Now the wooden floorboards in the basement were warped and uneven from the heat and the water. It was easy to trip in the dark, in spite of flash- lights, and the staircase wobbled and creaked. Objects were scat- tered all over the place. We entered the storeroom. It was a long room and the detectives led me to its far end. A pool of crimson blood had dried on the cement floor in front of some cardboard boxes. On the boxes themselves were more splashes of blood. Glued to a ceramic vase on the floor was a piece from a pair of dark blue Adidas jogging pants with their two white stripes. Shan had been wearing them. The fire had bonded the cloth to the ceramic.

Here Vijay had struggled. I gagged. Nina cried.

Why the basement? Vijay absolutely hated the basement and never came down here by himself. He was afraid of the dark, and the worn-out broken string on the bare light bulb was too high for him to reach. It seemed to me as though he had been trying to hide among the cardboard boxes in the far end of the darkest area of the basement.

But Dad had found him.

It had taken the firefighters an eternity to find the bodies. There had been one to two feet of water in the basement from the fire hoses, and the infrared equipment used for smoke-filled areas could not detect the heat from the bodies under the water. They had finally spotted a foot sticking up and taken out the bodies one by one. Vijay and Dad were found lying next to each other, in opposite directions. The handleless knife was next to Dad's body.

Looking for Answers

Raj had phoned Shan's mother and younger brother in India. Their initial reaction to the news was that it was a practical joke we were playing on them from Toronto. But finally the news sank in. They said they would come to Toronto immediately for the funeral rites. I was thankful that it was my brother who phoned them, I did not want to break such abhorrent news to Amma. Papa had passed away for some time now.

The next few days were hectic. I spent them with my sister and brother and Ranju, all of whom helped me with the things that needed to be done—the two funeral arrangements, the religious rites, talking to the insurance company.

Gary and Joe, the two detectives of the York Regional Police, came to visit me. Although friendly and sympathetic, they performed their duty first.

"You're sure we aren't going to find a boyfriend in the background?"

No, I replied, there was no one. Are you sure, they insisted. Yes, I was sure.

"You were lucky not to be at home. In cases like this, often the whole family is wiped out."

"Yes, " I said. "He would have liked to take Nina as well, and leave me with nothing."

"Were you able to find out anything more about the timing of the events?" I then asked.

"We think the fire started at about 6:15 in the basement. He did pour some gas in the family room before he went downstairs. Then he doused himself with lawn mower fuel before lighting it. We found both the barbecue lighter and the plastic gas can next to him. Your son died before the fire was started, we think, but we will know better after the autopsy."

I still didn't understand the timing—perhaps I was trying to analyze something that could not be explained logically. "It sounds like he was waiting for Nina and me, otherwise why would he wait till 6:15? He could have done it earlier. I left just before 5:00."

"Some kids say they saw Vijay on the bike around 5:30."

I found out later that Vi had called his friend Christopher, just after the *Simpsons* started on TV at six, but Chris had not been home. Chris's sister had not picked up the phone, but she had noticed that it was Vi's call. Was he trying to get help, or was it just a friendly call? What I really wanted to know was how long he had to suffer, and it was driving me insane.

"How did he kill Vijay?" I asked the detectives. Did he hold him from behind and slash his throat so that Vijay couldn't tell what was coming? I hoped this was true.

They both looked at me, hesitated, and said they didn't really know. I couldn't tell if they were not telling me out of kindness or if they *really* did not know. I wanted to know the truth, only the truth, even if it was of the worst kind.

"The knife we found next to him had a twelve-inch blade and was very sharp. The handle burnt off so we can't tell what make it was."

"All the knives I had were blunt, and I never owned twelve-inch knives. Mine were smaller."

So we came to the conclusion that he must have bought the knife earlier. Nina still contends that they said it was a butcher's knife. The memories are blurred already, but the thought of the knife is sufficient to trigger a mental chill in me even now.

"Your husband's wallet contained an ATM transaction receipt. He withdrew $80 Thursday morning, and we found only $54 left in his wallet."

I know Shan had not used the money for gas because we had just filled up the Toyota. He must have purchased the knife with it.

Friends and well-wishers dropped by and phoned. There were phone calls from all over the world. Somehow everyone we had known had found out about the tragedy. It was easy to cry from self-pity when people were around. It was truly difficult for most people to know what to say—they could not provide me with any hope, so they cried along with me. Some said short prayers for the departed. I remember the words that someone uttered in my ear, words that lifted my soul above the clouds: "Vijay is happy where he is—don't worry about him." And when that brought tears to my eyes I realized that it was Vi's suffering that had devastated me. But that thought, that he was happy where he was, would stay with me forever.

The next day the detectives told me the autopsies confirmed that Vijay had died first, of multiple slashes to his throat. The killing was an act of a man engulfed with rage. The boy's head was barely hanging by the spine. My husband had then thrown gas over his own body and set himself on fire. His skin had turned a marble of brown and beige, I was told.

At first, Vijay must have thought that Dad was just fooling around. I dearly wanted to believe that when this game turned into a nightmare, Vijay had been too busy defending himself even to think about fear. What torture it must have been for him, coming down to the dark basement to hide from his father, called by his angry voice, and finally being discovered. Nobody should have to suffer so, especially at the hands of his own father. The furnace room in the basement had only one entrance, and escape was impossible past the narrow entrance. Vi must have realized that, as he sat crouching in the dark.

The thoughts of that struggle jarred my soul. I could not bear them. They could not answer the whys. Why the rage with his own son, the son for whom he bought toys, the son he had loved with pride, the son who looked like him? About two years later, one of my spiritual gurus tried to pacify the torture in my heart. With kindness, he said, "Do you remember when your child was born? Did you not go through a lot of pain then? Did you recall that pain every time you saw him and think, Oh I went through a lot of suffering for this boy's birth? No, of course not. Similarly, he went through this suffering only to take on the next step in life's evolution. Do not worry, it is only to be free that he struggled. It happened, but it is over now."

According to Vedantic philosophy the *atma* (spirit) does not die. It was there before we were born. And because it was never born, it never dies. It always has been and always will be. Our bodies die in the same way as one discards clothing at night. But the spirit dons new clothes with every birth, to complete the accumulated and unfulfilled plans and desires of many previous births. And though we may not be born at the same place, we are in the same mind space as when we died. We go through many lives and get closer to liberation in each, assuming we have accumulated more good actions than bad ones.

This belief, that the spirit does not die, was critical to my survival and that of Nina's. It was only this knowledge that pulled us through the bleakest moments of our despair. Nobody could have saved us but ourselves. Who can possibly convey the enormously subtle aspects of one's life to another?

I wanted to see my son's body. I did not care what it looked like. I knew time would pass and the opportunity would not come again. The funeral parlor said they would embalm the face and I could come on Monday. Nina also wanted to see Vijay.

What we saw looked very little like Vi. The face looked plastic, like a doll's, his eyebrows had been painted on. He did not have proper eyelashes, though his hair was intact, and his new brush cut from last Tuesday, less than a week ago, was very apparent. We could not go close to him. There was a rope barrier around the body. Nina reached out and poked Vi's stomach, as she often did when they kidded each other, but she was shocked to feel his hard body. His neck was covered by a white cloth, so I could not see the massive cut I knew was there. Let him be, I told myself. It does not look like him in any case. The Vi I remember will be felt in my heart, sought in my memory. This one I do not want to carry with me at all.

My own neck ached, as if someone had cut it. I would feel that sensation many more times in the future, and instinctively my hand would reach out toward the right side of my throat.

One of our friends had identified the body, and I had been told that when Vi was pronounced dead, his eyes were open. The horrifying trauma of his ordeal had been evident in his wide-open eyes.

Now they were closed.

The Funeral

The two funerals were held at the same time, eight days after the deaths, for we had been waiting for Shan's family. The bodies were cremated, according to Hindu custom. I liked the idea of the spirit being released from its outer shell, purified and freed by the burning fire. Now my son could progress to newer grounds, and he was one step closer to liberation. How could I not be happy for him? He had done nothing wrong in his little lifetime. He had only given. And so I made peace with myself. I never thought about Shan at all. How his spirit would handle his crime was his own problem.

The words my daughter spoke at the funeral for her brother were especially significant to me. In her I admired the strength and courage to stand and speak in front of the many hundreds who had gathered. I couldn't have done what she did. She knew very well what tributes she wanted to pay to his memory, and I don't think anyone could have stopped her. I knew she was going to be okay. It was the eighth day since Vi's death and she had come a long way already.

Support from the many communities was overwhelming. Present at the funeral were all the teachers who had ever taught my son, his friends and their parents, two full busloads from Nina's and the neighboring schools, many school officials, well-wishers from the Indian community, my close friends, many of Shan's coworkers, and a large number of coworkers from my workplace. I cried more because of all the sympathy I was showered with, than because of Vijay's departure.

Nina spoke of her young brother with tenderness. She compared Vijay to the god Ganesh, who is the obstacle-remover form of the one God, the one Truth. Vijay had always been fascinated by Ganesh and had an altar in his room with Ganesh's statue. I remember the first time his grandmother asked him what he wanted when she came to visit him from India, and Vi had asked her for Ganesh's statue, nothing else. Nina in her speech captured Vijay's love for the god, and had called her brother "my little Ganesh." Through faltering speech and suppressed tears she satisfied her need to profess her undying love for her only sibling.

But afterwards, at home, in the coming months she would feel the loneliness without his chatter and his antics. Even now, several years later, on quiet evenings, she will ponder and commiserate over her loss, she will listen to his music or draw something in memory of him.

On my part, the practice of absentmindedly talking to him as though he were still alive has abated. It was natural for several months to say, "Vi, what do you want for dinner—" "Vi have you—" and not complete the sentence, realizing he was not present anymore.

Vijay had been a lively soul, known at school for making people laugh, for his love of sports and drums. He was on his way to getting a black belt in karate, he had learnt to play the Indian tablas. His little soul was gentle and tender, and it warmed my heart to think that in his way he could have helped to shape the world. His teachers and his classmates paid tribute to his sincerity and generosity. I know he had a spirit in him that would have made him grow up to be a reverent and responsible brother and son.

Vijay was never the price I was willing to pay for my freedom. His sacrifice for me was the offer of freedom. It is not his loss that brings tears to my eyes: it is that ultimate sacrifice that humbles me, that often shatters me completely.

Epilogue

Less than a month after the incident, I contacted Shan's workplace to find out whom he had counseled with. They would not release to me, or to the lawyers, any information—even whether he had actually presented himself for counseling. And when I called the hospital where he told me once that he had had an ECG when I had urged him to visit the doctor for a physical, there was no record to be found. He had obviously wanted me to believe that he had sought all the help necessary and if there was a problem, it was I, not he. His fear and shyness with the world contributed to his withdrawal from the necessary actions of the living body. The detectives searched for clues at his workplace, but did not find any explanations. There was a longish note he had written to me that I found in one of his work binders, in the middle of many empty pages. It acknowledged his behavior toward me, and how he would have improved had he been given another chance. He wanted to be forgiven. And yet, I found a long kitchen knife in the trunk of Shan's red Toyota. I could not help thinking about the Sunday when he took me for the drive up north.

With the funds I received from well-wishers, I set up a trust fund in Vijay's name to award students who excel in the arts at Ramer Wood Public School.

When I received the autopsy reports from the coroner's office, I learned that Vijay had scars on his cheek, on his chin, and on his chest. He also had two very deep cuts on the web between his fingers—on both hands. Vi had fought bravely and tried his best to defend himself. Shan died of smoke inhalation—it had taken him almost fifteen minutes to perish. They both suffered in their last moments.

Last year there was one piece of unfinished business. I had a great yearning to give Vi the purest, most precious rite of all, so that he would be truly blessed by the gods, and so that his rite of passage could be nothing but noble and sacred. There is a glacier high up in the Himalayas from which the sacred river Ganges commences its flow. I took his ashes there and released him from his last ties to this world, and prayed for him to move on.

For many of us living is an inharmonious, confused, and complicated affair, a chaotic roller coaster. But it does not need to remain that way. With experience and the hardships of life comes quiet wisdom.

How we struggle to keep balance, learn to compromise ourselves, and then wonder why we are still not happy! We give freely of ourselves until we can give no more, compromise until we can concede no more. Then one day when it dawns on us that life will pass us by as we endure our undeserved fate, we question our past, the decisions we took, and how we came to be where we are. We can marvel at the incomprehensible and follow each and every tangled thread of our bewildered lives, but cannot blame ourselves for the choices we made. They were right in their own accord, in themselves, at their time, at their place, and within the limitation of our incomplete knowledge. It is unfair to put them under any kind of scrutiny.

The day we shed our fears and move on, instead of lashing out at the injustice, and acknowledge that we have violated our good selves because of our faint hearts, we become rich with happy expression, guided by a natural love for the world. We flourish and evolve as we are meant to—and as do others who are with us.

And though we may pay a price in the struggle toward that harmony, we know that we are left with a heart that is more precious than what we left behind. The perfect world is not of mundane possessions or of mediocre living, but is the culmination of all experiences that slowly guides us on the path of being free and perfect, of being our most natural, unadulterated, and complete selves. How we need to pay tribute to that spirit in us, and not the world it lives in! And when the all-encompassing spirit is alive, the world becomes trivial. There are no more judgments, opinions, only a deep appreciation, an acceptance of all there is and all that is yet to come.

In the scheme of things, I see this incident as God's wish to expand my wisdom, and I wait for it to envelop my miniscule understanding. Sometimes I understand, but mostly I accept. Acceptance is his gift to Nina and me, vanquishing the small fears of our minds.

There is no doubt that my survival is a result of God's love. He prepared me well beforehand, giving me the knowledge of vedanta to navigate my way. There is no other knowledge that could have rescued me, given me the capacity to understand intellectually how and why things happen, to forgive, to love, and finally to embrace the largeness of Life. It has brought hardness to the head and softness to the heart.

This book is my tribute to Vijay. No one could teach me more about life than you. I am in your debt forever, Vi.

Acknowledgements

I have many to thank for who supported me throughout this tragic time.

Many thanks to Ramer Wood Public School's and Markville Secondary School's principal, staff, and teachers, and the parents of Vijay's classmates for their constant vigilance, presence, and guidance to the young ones; Vijay's friends and classmates for their touching gestures; Nina's closest in watching over her; the heartbroken firefighters who tried their best; the detectives—kind and sensitive in their line of duty; the York Regional Police #5 District Headquarters; and the staff of the Stouffville General Hospital.

Undying gratitude to my brother Raj and his wife Sweety for helping me bear; my sister Ranjana Didi for her unconditional support.

My warm thanks to close friends for their shoulder to lean on; and appreciation and recognition to colleagues and community for their kind support and understanding.

Respects to my timeless spiritual gurus, without whose knowledge and silent blessings, survival would have become unbearable

Grateful thanks to my editor, Moyez Vassanji, who patiently and painstakingly pieced together a perplexing story, and the kind and gentle Nurjehan, who preserved my heart throughout the writing of this ordeal.

To my precious daughter Nina, my world class coach and consultant: a generous and heartfelt thank you for being my cheerleader every step of the way!

RITA NAYAR has a university degree in psychology and a teaching certificate from the University of Sheffield, England. A senior corporate professional in Toronto, she is also an artist and a poet and teaches Vedantic philosophy. She lives in Markham, Ontario with her daughter.